DANIEL

People say time heals.

There is some truth in that, but
time itself doesn't heal; it just helps.

by **TAMMY CHUPP**

with excerpts from **RODNEY CHUPP**

ISBN 9781609201173
Printed in the United States of America

API
Ajoyin Publishing, Inc.
P.O. 342
Three Rivers, MI 49093
www.ajoyin.com

Please direct your inquiries to admin@ajoyin.com

ACKNOWLEDGEMENTS

This book is dedicated to my family. Rod, Chris, Becca, and Justus, thank you for walking with me through the healing process. Thank you for giving me grace as I have needed it, as I continue to walk toward wholeness in Jesus.

I want to thank Betsy Tacchella, Sue Werschky, Lynette Carpenter, Trish Konieczny, Rob Sisson, Pastor John Booko, and Angie Benn for their input with the editing process. Thank you, dear friends, for your gift of time and love. I also want to thank my cousin Brian Nusbaum for encouraging me to weigh my options, make a decision, and never look back. Thank you for your vote of confidence.

> *"The Spirit of the Sovereign LORD is on me, because the LORD has anointed me to preach good news to the poor. He has sent me to bind up the brokenhearted, to proclaim freedom for the captives and release from darkness for the prisoners, to proclaim the year of the LORD's favor and the day of vengeance of our God, to comfort all who mourn, and provide for those who grieve in Zion—to bestow on them a crown of beauty instead of ashes, the oil of gladness instead of mourning, and a garment of praise instead of a spirit of despair. They will be called oaks of righteousness, a planting of the LORD for the display of his splendor"* (Isaiah 61:1-3).

All scripture quotations are from the New International Version of the Holy Bible, unless otherwise stated.

FOREWORD

"Daniel" is an amazing story. Tammy and Rodney Chupp both wonderfully share not only their heart wrenching story, but also their hearts. It's clearly their desire for others to find the healing, hope, and help they have received.

If anyone is experiencing a "hard to understand" tragedy or overcome by grief yet want help, this book will give them hope; help them get back on their feet; show them how to treasure the good and look forward to better.

We often feel at a loss to know how to comfort and help those who have experienced painful tragedies and are grieving. Thank you for sharing your story – this book will help many of us to know how to be more compassionate and supportive.

Some people run from God after tragedy strikes and find only more hurt, pain, grief and sorrow. Yet you ran to Him in the midst of it all and found peace, purpose and joy. Yes, there is healing, help and hope for all who will turn to God in spite of what they don't understand. God has said He would never leave us nor forsake us and it is in situations that seem unbearable and impossible that this takes on a whole new meaning.

Through the sharing of your story we pray that many will connect to the faithfulness of God's grace. God's grace is His supernatural power and ability to handle things that are too difficult for us. It is strength that is far above and beyond our own. It is supernatural. It is not deserved. It is not earned. But it is given because He loves you. He provides it. May we all run to HIM and receive it.

– Duane & Jeannie Vander Klok,
Senior Pastors of Resurrection Life Church in Grandville, MI

" *Daniel"* is an extraordinary testimony of unconditional faith on God and His amazing power to heal the deepest wounds.

I strongly recommend this book, it is so real and profound. Thank you Tammy and Rodney for sharing your son's story. His 13 month life will impact millions to seek Jesus and to trust Him, even when it is impossible to understand.

I believe this book is an instrument in the hands of God to provide healing and restoration to multitudes. "

–Pastor Frank Lopez, Pastor - Jesus Worship Center, Miami Florida

" *A powerful story about coping with every parent's worst fear. One couple's love for each other, guided by God's invisible hand, gives all of us hope in our times of despair.* "

–Robert Sisson, President – ConservAmerica

" *In this life, the loss of a loved one brings tremendous hurt and pain, but the deepest pain of all has to be what our Father experienced in the death of His son. Rodney and Tammy have shared the most tragic pain any person can experience: the loss of their child in this world. Their story reminds us that thru any pain we bear, we have a Heavenly Father who is faithful to bring comfort, healing, and love. The Chupps have shared and lived a life proving that even thru the darkest hours, believing in each other and trusting our Savior is indeed the answer. Time eases the pain, but precious memories become even more precious when we are fully surrendered to His will and our hearts are open to His healing.* "*

–Marlin Stutzman - United States Congress, Indiana 3rd District

" *As I read "Daniel" I got lost in a multitude of emotions ranging from gut wrenching sadness to pure enlightenment and admiration. What an amazing and well written tribute to their son Daniel and their testament of faith. A powerful love story about their love for their son, their family and God which gave them the strength to find joy again.* "*

Karin Zona - Business Manager – Mark Zona, Inc.

from the author

" *Did you pick up this book because you have lost a child or a dear loved one and are looking for hope to move forward, someone whom you can relate to, or to find answers to some difficult questions? If so, continue reading my story. I believe it will touch your heart and help push you toward the next stages in your healing process. It is my desire that you will grow closer to God as you renew your trust and belief in Him.*

If you have never lost a child but know someone who has, I also wrote this book for you. You will understand more tangibly what it is like to lose a child or a close loved one, and you'll be able to speak life into those around you who have experienced that or other devastating losses. You might learn what to say to them . . . or what not to say.

If you are in ministry, counseling, or have a heart for people; if you want to be better prepared to support those who have experienced a devastating loss, this book is definitely for you.

I will take you on a journey. Allow me first to paint a picture of my perfect life. Then, walk with me through the tragic loss of my firstborn child. That loss is even greater than I could have imagined. My story doesn't end there. I will demonstrate to you the beautiful ways God pieced back together my broken heart and emotions until one day, many years later, I felt whole again.

I pray that as you read my story, you will allow God to speak to, touch, and heal your heart, no matter what level of disappointments you have experienced in life. "

CONTENTS

Chapter One

CHILDHOOD HOPES AND DREAMS

My childhood was wonderful in so many ways. I had no idea what lay ahead, that as my life unfolded, there awaited an event so wrenching, it would change things in a dramatic way . . . forever.

* * *

I grew up in a loving home in the seventies, where my parents taught me about life, God, and having fun. I was the oldest of four children, three girls and a boy. I didn't know until many years later that we would have been considered "poor." I had the world by the tail because my family knew how to have fun together, I knew my parents loved me, and family was important.

We kids were often a magnet to Dad when he was home. He didn't mind a bit. In fact, he usually gave us something to do, so we felt like we were *helping* him. I think, sometimes, we probably were a bit of a help. We would hand him tools while he was working on a project in the garage. We'd help do chores. We would help him shovel snow, or even shovel manure. Sometimes, he would let us help him push the lawn mower. We were really good at giving Mom messages, but my main memories of helping Dad were in the garden.

Dad would measure and make many long, even rows after the soil was cultivated. We kids would place the seeds in the soil, just as he instructed: about two to three inches apart for peas, beans, carrots, and beets, a little farther apart for corn. The onion sets would be placed "just so." Tomatoes and pepper plants were much farther apart. The cucumbers, zucchini, and squash were planted on small hills.

We helped keep the nice rows of produce weed free, and Dad would take the tiller between the rows to keep the weeds down. Mom occasionally reminds me that one day, as a very young girl, I proudly weeded the carrots. When I was done, there was not one weed left in that row . . . nor were there any carrot plants left. Dad surely chuckled and shrugged it off as a learning lesson. That's how he was—very patient. Everything was a potential teachable moment.

When it was time for harvest, we kids were always a part of the work, though I'm sure Mom and Dad did the majority of the actual work. We shelled peas, snapped beans, husked corn, washed cucumbers to prep them for pickling, sorted tomatoes for canning. You name it, we were right there helping and learning. Everything was a learning process, and we loved it. We loved learning about life, and we loved spending time as a family.

Matt and me playing near our garden while Dad husked sweetcorn.

Mom was generally around, except during the occasional seasons when she would wait tables a few nights a week. She was a stay-at-home mom like many moms in those days, at least the ones I knew. She was a busy lady. We shared in the housework. She always kept a tidy home. What I learned most from her was how to cook delicious meals from scratch, can and freeze our produce, and how to feed a family of six on a very tight budget. I loved being part of the process of the work she did for our family while Dad was at work as the town barber. My favorite thing I did with Mom was watching her can tomatoes and tomato juice. I helped some, though I was likely in the way more than anything. I took mental notes, because I knew someday I, too, would teach my children how to can tomatoes, as well as cook and many of the other things Mom taught me.

Mom tried to teach me to sew. I can sew a straight line, but not the cute and thrifty Barbie clothes she could make. I never really did pick up a knack for sewing, only the necessities like hemming pants, sewing on a button, mending a tear, and maybe making a simple pair of curtains.

Dad used to take us for hikes through the woods with our horse Lucky. All the kids would pile on the horse, and Dad would walk Lucky, a.k.a. Black Devil, moving branches and limbs as we went. It was always exciting and a bit scary if Lucky had to step over a log. We held each other tightly. Dad packed special treats (I'm guessing Mom actually did the packing, but we didn't know that at the time): a canteen of water, sometimes sandwiches and apples, and, typically, a few mini candy bars. We would stop and eat shortly after getting across the field and into the woods. We would then use the wrappers to mark a trail so we could find our way home. It worked every time! We always managed to find our way back home. What great memories!

Dad walking Lucky with several riders.

Soda pop and ice cream were special treats in our home, only to be enjoyed once a week. On Friday nights, Mom would pop up a batch of popcorn and divvy up a sixteen-ounce bottle of Pepsi between all of us kids. Dad would hold the popcorn bowl as we all gathered around him to feast on it. This was the only time we were allowed to eat in the living room. We were usually watching a show together. Saturday nights were for ice cream. One time, we even got cherry chip flavor, Dad's favorite. We figured our parents must have spent a lot of money on it. We were only allowed a little bit.

Every so often, Dad would make a trip to the feed mill to get grain for our two horses. I remember one time very specifically. I got to ride with him, and, for whatever reason, none of my siblings went. That meant I got Dad all to myself. That would have been enough for me, but when he got back in the truck after taking care of his business, he handed me a small package of M&M'S. A whole package—all to myself! I felt very special. I knew that Dad loved me, but I really felt it that day. (Now, I know that he was speaking my two biggest love languages—quality time and gift giving.) To this day, when I think of that trip to the feed mill, it gets me a little choked up.

As children, my brother Matt and sisters Marci and Alicia and I spent many hours outdoors. Since our parents rented a house on a small farm, we had the run of the place. We would play hide and seek in the wheat field, chase chickens, play for hours in the hay forts we made in the barn, and even play in the drainage culvert that ran under our road, which usually had a small stream of water running through. The culvert was probably about four feet round and seemed like the perfect size for us to play in and not be noticed by anyone. Our older neighbor boys would sometimes join us in play. Their house was nearby, and there were no other houses within a half mile or so. Another activity we would do on occasion was to pack a picnic lunch and ride our bikes down the road to a large tree. We would enjoy our picnic, until the ants found us. I'm guessing it was a tenth of a mile from the house, but it seemed like another world when we were there. We made many great memories at that little farm.

The electric fence was a bit of a challenge at times. We would try to go between or under the wires to avoid a shock. Oh, the surprise when we accidently touched it! Going past the electric fence was the only way to the barn, and that is where we often ended up. Looking back, Mom had to have enjoyed the peace and quiet while we played endlessly with few limitations.

When we were pretty small children, we all slept in one set of bunk beds in one of two bedrooms on the main floor of our farmhouse. Mom and Dad had the other bedroom. That worked well for many years. It wasn't until I was about nine or ten that Mom thought it was time to move a couple of us to a bedroom upstairs. Our old, drafty farmhouse had three more bedrooms upstairs. They were stifling hot in the summer and very chilly in the winter months. We depended on fans or an electric blanket. Prior to having an electric blanket, Mom used to warm the sheets with a hot cast-iron skillet. She would first warm it on the stove, then briskly rub it between the sheets, which made it so toasty. We kids would climb immediately into bed to enjoy the blessing of warmth and snuggle together to help keep each other warm.

Me and Matt sitting in Dad's barber chair after Matt's first haircut.

We often played "barber" on my dad's old barber chair. One day, Mom was babysitting my cousin Ed. I snuck the scissors out of her sewing basket and proceeded to give my brother and cousin a haircut. It was great. I knew Mom wouldn't approve of our version of playing house, so I carefully swept all the hair behind the chair and put the scissors back so she would never know. I was quite surprised later when she somehow found out what we did. I thought she must have been pretty smart to figure it out. Of course, the boys' hair was a disaster. Aunt Mary Alice, who is my godmother, was not amused when she arrived later to pick up her son. He was to be in a wedding the next week. I still didn't understand why it was such a problem. Thankfully, Dad fixed Ed's hair the best he could with his barbering skills. I don't remember Mom being asked to babysit Ed after that.

Every weekend, we would visit both sets of grandparents. That's just what we did, every week. Of course, my other aunts, uncles, and cousins would do the same. So we got to see our large extended family often. I grew up with fifty-four first cousins. We had good relationships, and we looked forward to seeing each other every weekend. I still have good relationships with my cousins to this day, and I love them dearly.

My family in the late seventies.

Mom's youngest sister, Jane, was only six years older than me. We often played together during our childhood. I have a close relationship with her that started when we were kids. We made Grandma Sobota's pantry / broom closet our playhouse. We would take M&M'S, divide them according to color, and "cook" our yellow corn, orange carrots, brown steak, green peas, and red tomatoes, then enjoy the fruits of our labor. She usually got to be the mom. We made snow forts in the winter, played in hay forts in the summer, rode bike, swam in the local pool, played endless hours with Barbies, and had many talks together as we grew up. When I was older, she let me tag along with her to the skating rink, where she taught me how to roller skate. I'm not sure taking me was her idea, but nonetheless, we skated together on a number of occasions. I thought her friends were so cool. We had so much fun together.

Because I had such a pleasant childhood, I couldn't wait to grow up to be a mom. I imagined life with my future husband through the lens of the "perfect" life I'd had growing up. I hoped for several children, and wanted to give them similar experiences. When I was a child, my hopes and dreams included: get married, have children, be a stay-at-home mom, and live happily ever after. As I grew, I pursued my dreams, and my dreams evolved.

. . .

"For you have been my hope, Sovereign Lord, my confidence since my youth" (Psalm 71:5).

"But Jesus called the children to him and said, 'Let the little children come to me, and do not hinder them, for the kingdom of God belongs to such as these'" (Luke 18:16).

"May the God of hope fill you with all joy and peace as you trust in him, so that you may overflow with hope by the power of the Holy Spirit" (Romans 15:13).

Chapter Two

EARLY MARRIED LIFE

During my teenage years, a lot changed from the time I had been a child, growing up in the small burg of Cecil, Ohio. In 1981 my family moved to Centreville, Michigan, due to Dad's job change. The move was an exciting adventure for us. The relocation was not only a fresh start with a lot of potential for our family, but it felt like a God-thing. Our family had eked by on Dad's barber income prior to his job at General Motors. With his new job, we not only had what felt like much more money, we also rarely got to see our Dad, who worked second shift. Things seemed very different from that point on.

I met Dawn Pahl (now Najmy) on my first day of junior high school in Centreville, along with many others who would become friends. Over the next few years, Dawn became my closest friend. She remains so to this day. It's a unique blessing to have known your closest friend for almost four decades. It's a relationship I greatly cherish.

After high school graduation, I pursued a nursing degree from our local community college with my parents' encouragement. I was the first person in my family to go to college. I really didn't think I was smart enough for college, but maturity made a big difference. I graduated with a better college GPA than high school GPA. I was probably the person who was the most shocked about that. I never did have a very healthy self-image, so I rarely believed in myself. That trend followed me long into adulthood, but God was faithful to prove otherwise to me.

I continued to have a lot of traditional ideals, though I eventually decided not to continue in the Catholic faith I had grown up in. I learned many things from my Catholic roots. My choice to leave the church wasn't intended to be a rejection of what I had been taught, though many of my extended family members, even my parents, seemed to receive it that way, at least for a season. My friends and relatives who are Catholic love, cherish, and value the traditional and religious experiences they have through their church. I appreciate that, yet I found a church that was a better fit for me in the ways I was seeking to understand and know more about God.

I grew up knowing about God. At an early age, my heart was committed to Him, though He seemed like a distant spiritual covering. I've always been a people pleaser, so naturally I was a God pleaser too. I was in awe of and respected Him, yet I felt like I was just one of many, many of His children—nothing special and probably a bother to Him. (Sadly, that's how I saw myself in relation to most people at that time in my life. I felt like I was a bother to them, and certainly nothing special. I tried oftentimes to stay invisible, so I didn't get in the way.) When I was sixteen, I learned it was possible to have a *personal relationship* with God. It was the difference from knowing *about* Him to actually *knowing* Him. Previous to that, my relationship with God was similar to knowing all about an actor or sports figure, but never actually meeting them. *Really* knowing God *and* having a personal relationship with Him changed my life and my perspective on life. I began to understand how very much God loved me, wanted me to talk to Him daily, and was delighted with being able to communicate with me.

I was nineteen when God led me to a wonderful group of believers at Grace Christian Fellowship in Sturgis. Over the years, I learned and grew so much there. That is where I met Rodney Chupp. We were young when we met and ultimately fell in love. We married twenty months after we started dating, at ages nineteen and twenty-two. I recommend being a little older when you make a significant decision like a lifetime partner, but we were pretty sure we "knew." We married on the warm, humid day of June 22, 1991, and our fairy tale began.

The first thing we learned is that married life is no fairy tale. Anyone who has experienced marriage knows that. I think people can be rather disillusioned in their ideals. In fact, we were. However, we still loved marriage and were beginning to piece together our ideal life. I graduated with my nursing degree just before our wedding and began working full-time as an RN on the night shift at Sturgis Hospital. Rod had taken the classes he needed at Michigan State and began working in his family's insurance agency. Every spare moment was spent on building our home. We lived in Rod's grandparents' basement while we worked on it. It was really Rod, not me, who did the work on our home. Many friends and family members helped us along the way, which made it possible for our small budget. Our home was incredibly simple and quite unfinished when we moved into it eighteen months later. We were so happy, especially because we were expecting our first child.

My kitchen had a stove, refrigerator, microwave, countertop, and sink. No cupboards—we couldn't afford those. Rod put a couple pieces of plywood and boards under the counter to form makeshift shelves. I made curtains to cover them, and that was the extent of our *cupboards*. A year later we got the smoke-and-water-damaged cupboards out of a home that had had a bad fire. They smelled terrible and didn't look good. I cleaned them up as well as I could. They worked and they were free! We were so happy to have them. We used those cupboards for five more years until Rod was able to make a beautiful kitchen, full of gorgeous oak cupboards, for me.

We had a borrowed chair, couch, and end table. The only furniture we owned was our bed, which Rod made, and the card table and chairs on which we ate every meal for years. Our floors were plywood. We had no (inside) doors on any rooms. We draped a blanket over the door frame of our bathroom to offer minimal privacy. Even our furnace was secondhand. Without all of the heat ducts in place, it was difficult to heat our house. Everything was simple, but we were happy. Eventually, we furnished our home with garage sale bargains or hand-me-downs from relatives. Though most everything we have today is secondhand, we have a great place. Most people would never know.

. . .

On July 18, 1993, our firstborn, Daniel Aaron Chupp, came into the world by C-section. A C-section was certainly not the plan, but we finally held our perfect baby boy in our arms. He was ours, and we were ecstatic! We were beyond content. We were one happy family.

We made the difficult choice to give up 70 percent of our income so I could quit my nursing job to be a stay-at-home mom. It was my dream. I never aspired to have a career. We sacrificed *so much* to make that happen. That choice isn't for everyone, but I knew it was right for me. I used cloth diapers, nursed my baby, and had most of his clothes gifted to us. Back then, we had a $20 budget each week for gas and groceries. That's what you have to do if your income is $170/week. Everything else went toward building the house and other living expenses. We had so little, but we made it work. It was worth the sacrifice because I was thrilled to be walking in the destiny I felt God had for me. We were *so* happy!

Being a parent is like nothing you can imagine, until it happens to you. Like marriage, it has its challenges for sure. Parenting is one of the most amazing blessings in life. Daniel was not only our first child, he was the first grandchild on both sides of the family and even the first great-grandchild for some of our grandparents. We took quite a few five-generation photos which are very precious. He never lacked for love and attention. He was so much fun and the delight of our lives, to say the least.

Front: *Great Grandma (Delila Chupp) holding Daniel, Great-great Grandma (Anna Troyer)*
Back: *Grandpa (Randy Chupp) and Dad (Rodney).*

I quickly adapted to being a stay-at-home mom. I couldn't imagine it any other way. Just like any parents, we delighted in every "first": his first smile and laugh, the first time he rolled over, the first time he sat up, when he first crawled, his first tooth, his first words, and, of course, his first steps.

First Christmas

I spent my days watching over him, playing with him, and meeting his needs. The evenings were "Daddy time." Rod was a very proud dad. He rocked Daniel to sleep every night as he sang "Amazing Grace" and other special tunes. When we went to church on Sundays, there was no need to take Daniel to a nursery. Rod held and snuggled him during worship time and took pride in caring for him during the rest of the service. It was a sacrifice for Rod to let others hold him, even the grandparents. That was his time. It was a special time.

Daniel was a very vivacious boy, full of life and joy. He was very affectionate. As active as he was, he still loved to snuggle with anyone that held him. He was a bit of a mama's boy, but would typically allow others to hold him and dote on him. That was a familiar part of his life. He was the center of attention anytime he was around his grandparents, aunts, uncles, great-grandparents, and many others. He was well-natured and frequently had a precious, very contagious smile. His almond-sliver, brown eyes sparkled when he smiled.

When he was seven months old, he was hospitalized with respiratory syncytial virus and pneumonia for five long days. I camped out beside his bed during that time. Occasionally, I would get right in the mist tent with him as I rocked him, nursed him, and comforted him. It was hard for us to see him so sick, with little energy. Around the fourth day, he began to pep up at times. The doctors and nurses seemed to stick around a little longer, as Daniel would entertain them. The way they responded to his charm made me think that that may have been the highlight of their shift. He was a special little guy, bringing such joy to anyone he came in contact with.

"Too big for his britches."

Auggie and Daniel

He learned to walk when he was 10½ months old. He was running shortly thereafter. He enjoyed shooting a regular basketball into the adult-sized rim that Rod created for him, which was about three feet off the ground. As he made his shot, he would say "ball" in his small, husky, toddler voice. He played contentedly most of the time while I caught up with my housework. He loved our large springer spaniel named Auggie, whom he frequently shared hugs with and patted as he pleasingly said "dog." Those were two of his eight words that he proudly practiced. We loved to hear him say them.

One memorable day, Rod was painting something in the garage with dark green, oil-based paint. Daniel had been playing in the yard, in sight of Rod. Without Rod realizing it, Daniel made his way into the garage and found the paint. He began exploring the stir stick, consequently dripping paint on the cement floor and on his shoes, when Rod realized what was happening. By then, we had a permanent reminder on the garage floor of our busy little boy.

I would occasionally stop at Chupp Insurance Agency for a short visit when I was in town for groceries. Rod worked there with his father, Randy; his grandparents Menno and Delila; and a few other hired staff. On a few occasions I left Daniel there while I made a quick trip to the store. Daddy loved showing him off there, and Grandma Chupp enjoyed spoiling him. On one occasion while we were there, Daniel walked around the corner and attempted to go down the hallway, out of sight. I firmly called his name and told him to come back. He stopped, looked and me, and came back toward me in obedience. That was not always his initial response to correction, but it was that day. For the most part, he was well behaved. One of the customers remarked what great parents we must be to have a child that listened so well. It was a proud moment for sure.

Daniel's first birthday was a special event with aunts, uncles, grandparents, great-grandparents, and other extended family. His grandparents spoiled him with a toddler-sized rocking chair, a wagon, a little toddler trike, and several additions to his wardrobe, including a little three-piece suit. Like any toddler, he enjoyed the wrapping paper, yet paid little attention to the gifts. He loved the attention he got from the many people who celebrated with him that day. We gave him his own cake to dig into, and he shortly became covered with chocolate frosting from his belly to the top of his head. Boy, did he have fun! There was a lot of laughter and so much joy that day.

 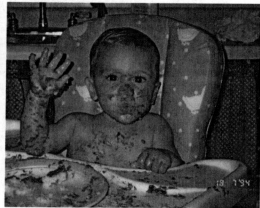

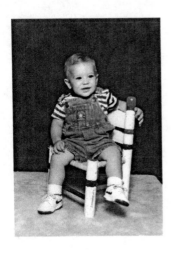

Shortly after Daniel's first birthday, we discovered we were expecting again. Life was so perfect. I couldn't imagine it could be any better. I was living my dream!

. . .

> "Take delight in the Lord, and he will give you the desires of your heart" (Psalm 37:4).

> "He will yet fill your mouth with laughter and your lips with shouts of joy" (Job 8:21).

> "Godliness with contentment is great gain" (I Timothy 6:6).

Chapter Three

PERFECTION STOLEN

I was nearly eight weeks into my pregnancy when I began having some light spotting. After seeing our doctor, I was encouraged not to do any heavy lifting and was told things would probably be fine. I had to avoid lifting Daniel. The spotting was slowly improving.

We were continually working on our house and making small improvements as we were able. This particular week, it was time to backfill the dirt against the basement walls. We had finally saved enough money to do it after living there for a year and a half.

To my delight, while garage sale browsing that morning, I found a set of bunk beds for $35. I was probably getting ahead of myself a bit, but I was pretty sure I *needed* to have them since I was expecting our second child. I asked the people to save them for me, and I'd be back with the money and a truck. They agreed to wait for my return.

I went home and told Rod about the deal that I couldn't pass up. He agreed to get the money out of our "emergency fund." I asked him to watch Daniel since I knew I wouldn't be long. I was so excited about my find that I wasn't thinking of all he would be busy doing that morning. I took his truck, and off again I went to town. I was probably smiling all the way there. I was more than delighted at the idea of adding a second child to our family.

. . .

The following section is Rod's perspective:

It was Labor Day weekend, a perfect time for labor. This was one of those rare opportunities which afforded me the opportunity for larger projects on the house. Approximately a week before Labor Day 1994, a client was in the office discussing his excavation business. The suggestion came that I should have this gentleman backfill around our home. I was hesitant. I considered the idea, however, because money continued to be tight, but later wondered where that apprehension really came from. We agreed to have the gentleman come to our home on Saturday and complete the desired work. Once the decision was made, I had great anticipation for the upcoming project.

The day came, and the excavator arrived. The driver began his work, and it was amazing how quickly things started to change. Progress can quickly be made with the collaboration of heavy equipment. Tammy arrived home from her trip to town visiting garage sales. She asked if she could take the truck and return to town for a set of bunk beds she was excited to buy. That suited me fine. She then asked if I could watch Daniel while she was away. I was busy, but loved having my son with me. I also knew it would not take long for a quick run into town. Without much thought I said, "Yeah, that's fine. I'll watch him." One should always consider his answer before responding.

As mentioned, Daniel was a happy little guy who was great at playing and entertaining himself. We had moved the doghouse to the middle of the back lawn due to the work we were doing that day. Daniel was playing with Auggie down behind the house, within sight near the doghouse. He would throw a medium-sized red ball, one of his favorites, into the doghouse and then retrieve it. He was doing this very happily, and he was very content. It was interesting how careful Auggie was while around Daniel. He would run and act rambunctious until Daniel and he would come into contact. At that point, Auggie would become very cautious and careful. It was a beautiful day. I was getting a lot of work done on the property. Daniel was enjoying the dog, the ball, and the doghouse. Things were great.

Heavy equipment can only get so close to stationary items. Due to this, there was a fair amount of dirt that was still heaped around the trees in the area soon to become a lawn. In an effort to complete all the work I could as quickly as I could, I decided to use a hand hoe to pull the dirt away from the trees. Then, if there was enough dirt, the dozer could drop its blade and spread it out. If it was a smaller amount of dirt, I could just spread it out by hand. While I stood at one particularly large oak tree, the thought raced through my mind, "I should go check on Daniel." I reached to pull one more clump of dirt and saw a bee come up out of the ground. Having had allergic reactions to bees as a child, my immediate thought was to eliminate the bee so he wouldn't be tempted to take his anxiety out on me. It took me a few moments to accomplish this feat. There are times in life when a few moments can make all the difference. This would be one of those times.

The events of the next few moments—those hours and days—have remained in my mind all these years. Particularly the next few moments have become etched in my mind in a way I cannot explain. I hope you do not fully understand, for if you do, I'm also sorry for what you too have experienced to have gained that understanding. Upon exterminating the bee and pulling the last couple of small mounds of dirt, I turned to go check on my son. I could not believe my eyes. Daniel was nearly halfway to me from where he had been playing. He looked like a little trooper on a mission. He had successfully negotiated the incline of a small hill and was coming my way. Usually, this would be a wonderful sight. *Not this time.*

The bulldozer had done most of its heavy earth moving. In fact, the job was very nearly complete. The operator was simply back-grading the freshly moved earth for a nice, even, final grade. Again, this would normally be a welcomed sight, one that would seem a blessing at the end of a long task . . . but not at this moment.

Daniel was coming toward me, and the bulldozer reversed its motion. Time seemed to stop. I could not imagine the two would collide; surely the operator would see him. I tried to move, but couldn't cover that much space quickly enough. My first thought was to yell "Jesus," but the word "NO!" came out of my mouth as I ran. The driver could not hear me over the roar of the machine. I watched as the machine continued in reverse. I saw the dozer bump my son, saw him lose his balance, and watched in horror as he disappeared under the machine.

I reached the dozer and had the driver stop. I was yelling, "My son, my son!" The driver asked, "Where is he?" I cried, "Under the dozer," as I feverishly pointed downward. The operator yelled, "No, no!" and pulled ahead. The only hope had been that Daniel fell between the tracks which supported the weight of the machine on which it drove. That was not the case. There are some things you simply cannot remove from your mind.

I sympathize with those who have witnessed the atrocities of war and other extensively emotional experiences. I don't begin to know how to write what I experienced. I'm not sure. It was awful, and yet there was a sense of "this can't be real" that overshadowed everything from that moment on for quite some time. I suppose it was some form of shock. I know God created us with the ability to deal with the unthinkable, for a time, when we must.

I picked up my son's lifeless body. He made no attempt to breathe or move. While his small body looked perfectly fine, he had severe trauma to his head, and I knew he was gone. I remember thinking, "Do you know what this means? Do you know what has happened?" I began yelling, "Breathe, in the name of Jesus! Breathe, in the name of Jesus! Breathe, in the name of Jesus!" At this, he began to breathe. Now, I have had medical professionals explain why this occurred, but I believe it was a divine intervention. Why the Lord would intervene at that moment and not earlier, why He would hear my prayer but would not have stopped this from happening, why, why, why . . . I do not know. I am convinced I may never know. My son breathed all the way to the hospital.

The dozer operator drove my car and took us to the hospital. Calling an ambulance was not even a consideration, as we had accidently cut the phone line earlier while moving dirt. We had no cell phones at that time. As we neared town, a police officer saw us and must have realized we were headed toward the hospital. Sergeant Ives, who later became a friend, drove in front of us with his lights on, clearing a path as we approached the hospital. We slid to a stop, half over a curb, and I ran into the emergency room with my son in my arms.

All of this had happened so fast. I gave them Daniel's small, limp body and began trying to gather my thoughts. I quickly realized I didn't want to gather my thoughts. I didn't want to be in reality. I couldn't imagine this was really happening. How would I reach Tammy? How would I reach my parents? Who should I call? God can heal. Surely He would do a miracle. Everyone was out of town, and I didn't know what to do! My pastors were even gone. Who should I call? I called a friend from our church. I can only imagine how I must have sounded. I was crying and babbling in half sentences. He, in turn, called a couple more friends and my cousin Rich Miller, who was like my brother. He also contacted the lead elder of our congregation. That gentleman played such a major role in the hours—and years—that followed. He has turned into one of my best friends and mentors in life. I am truly eternally indebted to my good friend Bill Tacchella. I called my uncle and aunt's house and explained that I didn't know how to reach Tammy. Aunt Carol said she would go find her. Then for a little while I was alone and devastated. How could I have allowed this to happen? How could I allow my perfect little child, the apple of my eye, Tammy's whole life and existence at that point in time, to be hurt? How could life go on if this didn't turn out well?

I remember having a nurse ask me my name. Upon realizing my name was Chupp, she inquired if I knew Tammy Chupp. When I told her Tammy was my wife, she got a very sick look on her face and said, "This isn't Tammy's son?" Upon my reply, she bolted for the room in which they were working on Daniel to relay the news. It felt like a new level of shock came over the team. Tammy had worked at our small community hospital for a few years before Daniel was born. She knew many of the nurses and doctors there. This made the situation very personal for the medical team who were doing all they could for our toddler son. When the nurse came back out, I asked her how

Daniel was doing. She didn't really answer. I asked twice more, and she very reluctantly told me, "You need to prepare Tammy for the worst." What a blow. I began to sob all over again, and I think she wished she hadn't responded. I was glad she was honest with me. I was bouncing between standing in faith and sinking in hopelessness. The news seemed to confirm the reality of what I had observed. This was sheer horror!

(End of Rod's account.)

. . .

I was thrilled to return home with my purchase. When I got home, I couldn't figure out where Rod and Daniel had gone, but I figured they'd be back soon. Things looked different outdoors, but I noticed they had left with more work to be done. I started making lunch.

When I heard a knock on the door, I was surprised. We rarely got visitors. It was Rod's aunt Carol, which was even more of a surprise. Before I could tell her that Rod wasn't home, she told me I needed to come to the hospital with her. I didn't understand when she told me Daniel had been run over by the bulldozer. I understood her to say Rod's dad had been run over. (I'm not sure how that misunderstanding happened, but sometimes I think it was the mercy of God, as we made that seemingly *long* drive to the hospital.) My first thoughts went to Rod and how traumatized he must be—enough so that he forgot the diaper bag. I grabbed it and a fresh bottle. Off to the hospital we went. I prayed all the way for Randy—the wrong person.

When we arrived at the emergency room, I found Rod and asked, "How is he?" I was referring to my father-in-law, whom I thought was the accident victim. I had not remembered that my in-laws were out of town that day. Rod said, "I don't know. They won't let me see him." I was purposing to be very strong for him, knowing he would need support. At some point, I looked down and realized I was still holding the diaper bag in my hand. I looked around and didn't see Daniel. So I asked, "Where is Daniel?" At that point, Rod looked at me like I was losing my mind. I could see by his expression and the dark confusion is his eyes that he was more than puzzled by my question. I asked again, this time more insistent and scared. He breathlessly said, "Tammy! . . . He's in there!"—pointing at the ER room. Once I realized it was my baby that had been in the accident, my knees went weak. The blood drained from my face. I could no longer stand.

When Rod recalls this moment, he said he realized his full guilt when I arrived and was confused about what had happened. He remembered, "There stood my wonderful, loving wife and dedicated mother . . . with a diaper bag and bottle for our son. I had to tell her it was Daniel. I will never forget the anguish and pain I saw in Tammy's eyes. The feelings are hard to attempt to describe. There was my wife, the love of my life and one of the strongest people I have ever known, collapsing from the news I had to explain."

Between the ER nurse, Gloria, and my wrecked husband, I was held up until they could get a wheelchair. By that time, I had begun loudly demanding answers. "How could this have happened? Why? How is this possible?" About as quickly as the wheelchair came to support me, I found myself in a private room with Rod and a couple of nurses. They whisked me out of the lobby very quickly, as to divert a scene. I couldn't process. I couldn't think. I wanted to know answers. I wanted to see my baby. How was this happening to me? It wasn't happening to me, was it? . . . It was.

Questions were flashing through my mind, and I wanted to demand that someone explain everything to me, because there was no way that this could possibly be happening. I was angry. I was so angry! In a split second, something stopped my words. I couldn't speak, and I heard God say to me in a firm tone, "Stop! Stop and think about what you are saying. Stop blaming! Rod is already feeling badly enough. He doesn't need you to do this to him. Just stop!" (I will never forget those exact words.) My head was spinning. My thoughts were going a million miles per hour. At that point, I couldn't talk, because I was having too hard of a time processing my thoughts. I sat back, took a deep breath, and began to sob. I never asked those blaming how or why questions again. I simply knew that what happened, happened, and there was nothing I could do to change it. At that moment, I chose to forgive. I forgave what I didn't even begin to understand. That choice stopped a wedge from attempting to work its way into our relationship in a threatening way. At the time, I had no idea of the significance of my choice. It would save my marriage.

Rod and the nurses were talking to me, but I didn't hear or process a word they said for some time. At some point, I tried to pull myself together and gather my thoughts. I then became insistent that I see my son. I didn't realize how bad off he was. They weren't about to let me see him like he was. A medical helicopter was on the way. The thoughts in my head were probably spinning about as fast as the blades on the chopper. I was praying. I knew he would be okay. I *knew* he would. He *had* to be.

About a year earlier, Daniel had been dedicated at our church. At some churches, people baptize their babies. In our church, we dedicate them. That means that we, as parents, vow before our friends and family that we will raise our child in a loving way, teaching him about Jesus and showing him the way

Jesus loves others. When Daniel was dedicated a year prior, a prophetic word was spoken over him. "Daniel will impact many people for the kingdom of God. He will have a great influence on the hearts of people. Because of him, many people will come to know the goodness and grace of God." I didn't write those words down at the time, but they still ring in my head. That is how I knew Daniel couldn't die. If God said it, it had to happen. And I knew those words were from God. I had felt it in my core.

Daniel's dedication. August 1993

There were several friends that heard about the accident and showed up in the Sturgis Hospital Emergency Room to support us. Thank God for our church prayer chain. I was blessed to have their support, but I couldn't look at them or talk to them. It seemed I had very little peripheral vision that day. It was the Saturday of Labor Day weekend, and both sets of our parents were out of town. There was no way to get ahold of them. This was before the convenience of mobile phones. Rod's cousin Rich was at the hospital with us and tried to help us figure out what to do. We desperately needed advice and wisdom. Where was our family? Somehow we had to get ahold of our parents. Through the chaos of thoughts and emotions that were whirling in our minds, we prayed.

Rod's parents were an hour and a half away in the Fort Wayne, Indiana, area for the day with Rich's parents. Rich was thinking strategically when he said, "My dad likes to eat at Cracker Barrel. What are the chances that they could be there eating?" Slim to none, we thought. He looked up the number to the Cracker Barrel restaurant in Fort Wayne. He called and asked if they could page to see if certain guests were there because of an emergency. The restaurant management cooperated. Guess what? They were there and had just been seated! Rich was able to speak to them directly and relay the horrifying news. Of course, they immediately left to head to Bronson Hospital in Kalamazoo, Michigan, a more than one hundred-mile drive, to which our son would be flown.

My parents were camping at a remote campground with no electricity several hours away. I thought we could call the people's home that owned the campground and at least leave a message, hoping that sometime over the weekend they would check their messages. Rod called the house, and to our surprise, their daughter answered. She had just stopped briefly at the house to pick up a few supplies and was heading back to the campground. It was another miracle that we caught her. She was able to relay the message immediately and my parents also headed north right away. Thank God! Rod and I were both in our early twenties and really needed the wisdom and support of our parents. We learned later that while my parents made the three-hour drive to the hospital, they wondered what had happened and what Daniel's injuries were. All they had been told was that there had been an accident, and that Daniel would be flown to Bronson Hospital. They had no idea the injuries were life threatening.

Sometime after the contacts were made, the helicopter came to pick up our baby. We hadn't seen him yet! We waited. It had already been an eternity. Suddenly, we realized they were wheeling him down the hall briskly on the way out the door to put him in Air Care. We hollered at them, "Wait! We have not even been allowed to see or touch our sweet boy." The medics stopped. They looked at each other in a knowing way and agreed to give us just a few seconds. When I saw him, I didn't recognize him. His head was one big bandage. What little of his face that was revealed was unrecognizable due to inflammation. "My baby!" I said with barely a whisper as I touched his soft, swollen face. I began to hug him, but the medics once again started wheeling the cart as one said, "We have to go." There was no time. There was no convincing them to give us more time with him. I didn't want to let him go, but I had no choice. Rod and I watched him go around the corner. We had barely seen him for a few seconds. Paralyzed in fear and the agony of our emotions, we held each other and sobbed. What was happening to our baby?

Rod and I were both in shock. Now what? We had no idea what we were doing. Thank God, our dear friend Bill, who is about the age of our parents, was there. He told us he would drive us to the hospital, over an hour away.

That was a godsend for many reasons. It was a *LONG* drive. On the way there, Rod and I cried endless tears. We went back and forth from thinking he would make it and not be paralyzed . . . to asking God to save his life, even if he was paralyzed . . . to thinking there was no way he could make it. Bill was in the driver's seat giving us the space we needed while we sat in the backseat and held each other. He only shared his thoughts or advice when we asked for it. Boy, did we need his wisdom. As Rod and I talked over the situation, we always came back to the idea that "he has to make it," because God had spoken a word over him, and it hadn't happened yet. We held each other's ice-cold hands and had to remind ourselves to take deep breaths.

We arrived at Bronson Hospital, and another long phase of waiting began. Again, many friends showed up to be a support. We had them as a distraction from the waiting, yet it was all a blur. Another blessing was that my sister-in-law Karen was working at that very hospital. She came to be with us as soon as she got word. She called my brother Matt, who was working on building his house with his friend Rob. They both came to the hospital. Later, Rob would pick up my sister Marci, who was working locally, and bring her to the hospital. The support system we had was amazing and such a blessing. I am very thankful to those who chose that way to show us they cared.

After what must have been at least an hour, a doctor came out to tell us Daniel wasn't going to make it because his spinal cord had been severed at the neck, and he was brain dead. They were only keeping him alive through life support measures. We were asked the hardest question I've ever had to answer. "Do you want us to stop lifesaving measures, or put him on permanent life support?" The next hardest question was, "If we stop life support, do you want to donate any of his organs?" *WHAT?* How could I possibly answer those questions?

Our parents had not yet arrived at the hospital, but we knew they were on their way. Yet, we needed to make a decision. We couldn't keep waiting. It could be another hour until they arrived. Once again, we turned to Bill for wisdom. After hearing his thoughts and thinking and praying about it for what felt like a long time, we made the decision to stop life support and donate Daniel's organs. To say that was a really, really hard choice is an understatement. We knew that God could have already healed him after hours and hours of praying, and we knew that God could breathe life back into him at any moment. But He didn't. Our son Daniel Aaron Chupp slipped into the arms of Jesus on September 3, 1994, at only 13 ½ months old. I didn't know if I could recover from the most devastating moment of my life.

• • •

I wondered if it was possible to cry more tears, but we cried many more tears that evening. We were disappointed to learn that Daniel's organs couldn't be donated because he had been oxygen deprived for too long. They removed all of the tubes and bandages to make him presentable for us to say goodbye. My parents arrived during that time, and we had to tell them the horrific news. They never expected to hear the tragic update when they arrived. We were taken into a private chapel room, and after what seemed like an eternity, they brought our lifeless baby to us to hold, to kiss, and to say goodbye.

Rod's parents arrived after we were in the chapel room with Daniel. Their worst nightmare was confirmed.

We all got to spend time holding Daniel, knowing it would be the last time. There were many, many tears. The hospital staff was amazing, giving us plenty of time with him. After nearly an hour, we knew we couldn't go on forever. We needed to give our final kiss and hug and say goodbye. Again, one of the hardest things I've ever done was to walk out of that hospital and go home that evening, without our firstborn son.

We would soon find out there would be very little sleep for us that night. Just more tears—tears from the depth of our soul. Perfection was stolen.

• • •

"I cried out to God for help; I cried out to God to hear me" (Psalm 77:1)

"Out of the depths I cry to you, Lord. Lord, hear my voice. Let your ears be attentive to my cry for mercy" (Psalm 130:1-2).

"They cried out to the Lord in their trouble, and he delivered them from their distress" (Psalm 107:6).

Chapter Four

THE NEXT
THREE DAYS

That first evening after the accident, we stayed with Rod's parents so we didn't have to go back to where the accident happened, just yet. We were still numb and in shock. How is it that my exciting morning had turned into the worst thing I could ever imagine? I was in the depth of despair, and it was only the beginning. In many respects, my life had been perfect. Perfect! What had happened? How was God allowing this to happen to us? Did we do something wrong? How could we deserve this? Was God who I thought He was? What did I believe? What about that word spoken over Daniel? I had so many questions. Who was going to answer them? My mind raced. I couldn't concentrate.

Our church youth group had gone on a mission trip and fun outing for the Labor Day weekend. When our pastor Ross Gerber and his wife Jennifer heard the news, they immediately returned from the trip with Rod's sister Shelly and my sister Alicia, who were both part of the youth group. The Gerbers know all too well the loss of a child, after having lost their two and a half-year-old daughter Jade to leukemia eight years earlier. To our surprise, they showed up at my in-laws' doorstep at eleven thirty that evening with Rod's sister Shelly. We embraced and the tears too easily broke loose again. We talked, cried, and prayed together for hours. We asked them many questions. Their answers were something like this: "We don't understand it either. There are many things we don't understand that God allows, but we know He is sovereign. We need to choose to trust Him, even when we don't understand." Jen shared about having a decisive moment when she chose to trust, in spite of all of her questions and pain. I let those thoughts filter through my mind for a while.

Ross shared how couples who lose a child often struggle in their marriage, and a great deal of those marriages end in divorce. He strongly encouraged us that evening before they left to make a decision or a vow that we would not allow this tragedy to devastate our relationship. He and Jen also challenged us in what we really believed about God. Did we trust Him or not? They beautifully prodded us to face and answer that question that evening. Rod and I both agreed that we did trust God, despite our many questions. We also knew, and made a choice, to continue to believe that God is sovereign. We stood on that truth that evening, and that's what we clung to in order to begin our journey through the healing process. I had so many questions for which I needed answers, questions for which only God knew the answer. Regardless, the decision was secured. Rod and I chose to trust God.

Finally, I placed my head on a pillow sometime after three o'clock in the morning. I wanted sleep. I wanted to close my eyes and forget everything. Maybe I would wake to realize it was all a horrific dream. I simply didn't want to have to think. But sleep did not come . . . for hours. My mind and emotions tortured me. I sobbed and sobbed. I finally drifted off to sleep for a short time.

. . .

Do you trust God? We have learned that being able to lay our burdens down at the feet of Jesus and really trust Him has made a big difference in our lives. I can't imagine what it would feel like to not know the comfort and peace of a loving God. If you have never given yourself over to Him, I encourage you to do so. Trust the same Jesus who has walked us through our deepest pain. Without Him it seems there is little to no hope of peace and comfort. Without Him, we would have to bear our burdens on our own. That is a big job. He is willing to carry our burdens and even carry us at times. Consider giving your burdens to Jesus and trusting Him in that way.

. . .

When I awoke the morning after the accident, I realized it was, unfortunately, not a dream but a very real nightmare I was living. My mother-in-law, Rosa, was awake and had coffee waiting for me. We both cried again. So many decisions were ahead. There were so many things to process.

It was Sunday morning and I wanted to go to church, mostly so I could get my mind off of everything, but also so I could lose myself in worship. I tried to get ready. I attempted to put on makeup. There was no use. I couldn't stop the tears, let alone the ugly cry. I knew I was not ready to face people and the questions.

There were a few phone calls and a few visitors that morning. With each face and each voice, the dam of tears would burst forth again. I didn't think I could have any tears left to cry, but that was only the beginning of them. There would be many more to come—many more.

I had to call my best friend Dawn, who lived nearly five hundred miles away. She was at church, so I left a message with a friend of hers. I could barely get the words out. Tears and a flood of emotions constantly choked out my words. What in the world was I going through? I still couldn't believe this was real. But it was. Dawn phoned me back a few hours later, and I had to tell her the hell that was happening to me. We cried together more than we talked.

That afternoon and evening, there were many visitors and a lot of food. I couldn't eat. I could barely even drink. I was nauseous and had physical pain in the pit of my stomach that wouldn't go away. We had to make a trip to the funeral home to make some arrangements. I didn't know what to do. What twenty-five-year-old buries her thirteen-month-old baby? What twenty-five-year-old makes funeral arrangements for her firstborn and only child? How is one supposed to think, let alone plan a service and make important decisions? I didn't know. But somehow, together with Rod and our parents, we did it. We made all of the necessary decisions and returned to my in-laws' home in numbness . . . with more food—that I couldn't eat.

As I thought about funeral plans, I felt compelled to write some words to share, though I didn't think I'd have the strength to read them myself. We found out that Rod's cousin Greg Miller, who was an important spiritual mentor, was on his way home from Costa Rica, where he was living at the time. We decided to ask Greg to share my words at the funeral. (The words I wrote are in Appendix A.)

We also learned that our senior pastor, Vic Hildebrand, was trying to find a flight home from the Dominican Republic, where he was on a three-month mission. It meant the world to us to know the love and support of loved ones all around. We needed to glean from their strength, wisdom, and maturity. We felt so cared for.

Some neighbors that I had never met stopped by to bring a large ham. Dan and LaVonne Borgert grieved for us and did all they knew to do to be a comfort and support. We realized that Dan and our Daniel even shared the middle name Aaron. It was a special moment of bonding. From that point on, their family has been a special part of our lives.

We returned home to sleep in our own bed that evening.

* * *

As much grief as I was experiencing, Rod seemed to be dealing with it at a deeper level. He was there when the accident happened. He turned just as our adventurous little boy ran behind the excavator. He had that visual image of a large, earth-moving bulldozer engulfing our small son under its treads etched in his mind. The horror and guilt were overwhelming for him. He began turning his thoughts, feelings, and emotions inward. It was torturous for him, but that was the way he dealt with the devastation of losing his firstborn and only son. He withdrew from me. He felt as though he had betrayed me, and he could hardly face me, let alone speak about the accident and his feelings. (That went on for a year.)

Evening two after the accident, I slept! Thank God! But when I woke, I had to remember all over again that the baby I had just weaned was no longer mine to hold, kiss, laugh at, smell, be proud of, snuggle with, and to dream of future goals for. There was so much loneliness in the atmosphere of our home. I wandered around aimlessly that morning. It was the day of the viewing. I scanned my closet for something appropriate to wear. It was difficult to think. I walked back to the kitchen. I was breathing, but nothing else came naturally for me. I was lost in my own home. My mom stopped by after buying me a suitable dress to wear for the funeral. It would do. The few times I wore it in later months, I despised it. I eventually gave it to Goodwill so I didn't have to look at it again.

Auggie was moping around, acting very melancholy. It seemed that he was missing Daniel and somehow *knew* he was gone. That was another difficult reminder to us.

It was Labor Day—a day when many people have off work, go picnicking, camping, or just hang out with friends and family to relax, have fun, and forget about the cares of the world. Not me. I wasn't having fun. And I honestly didn't know how the rest of the world could just go on as if everything was fine. I sincerely didn't get that. Didn't everyone know? My son died! My only child was gone! My world had come to a screeching halt. How could they laugh or have fun? I didn't understand. I think that is a very surreal thing that many people face while going through a tragedy. When something consumes your whole world, how does it not consume everyone else's? But it doesn't. Life goes on.

On that Labor Day, we drove to the funeral home in preparation to begin receiving friends and family as they looked at our tiny son in his tiny casket. When I walked into the building, I froze. It was difficult to make myself walk into the next room to see him. It felt difficult to fill my lungs with air. There was a heaviness on my chest. I felt very anxious. How could I look at my baby lying there, lifeless, after not seeing him for two days? Eventually, I gathered enough nerve to go in. The sight of him in his brown, three-piece suit he got for his first birthday brought me to my knees. Once again, I couldn't stand without support, and the floodgates opened. My baby! That's my baby! There was nothing about it that felt right or natural. I prayed silently, "God, please take this nightmare away. I can't bear it!"

Eventually, I pulled myself together and prepared myself for the hundreds of people that would soon be walking through those doors: the people that were coming to support and encourage us, to hug us, and to somehow create closure in their own minds. One thing was very evident to me through those few days: we were very loved and had a lot of support. I saw many friends and relatives that I expected to see. I saw some people that I never expected to see. I looked for some people that didn't make it. It was a strange thing.

The youth from the church arrived back in town. Many of that group came straight to the funeral home to express their shared grief. I felt so badly that our tragedy put such a damper on their "fun" weekend.

We received many, many hugs that day. Most everyone was so gracious, not knowing what to say, and it was all right. I understood. I had been in their shoes many times, not knowing what to say to the loved ones of the deceased. One distant relative came and felt she needed to share her "wisdom" with me. She had also lost a child. She said, "I know this is really hard for you, but this isn't the hardest part." *Did she just say that?* I couldn't believe my ears. I did not want to hear that or know that. I couldn't process how it could possibly get harder. I was immediately angry! If there would have been bouncers there, I would have had her thrown out! However, I would later learn that she was right. God's grace was with me to give me strength and help me get through another tearful day. With each new face we encountered came a new reason to remember and a new reason for tears. Rod was numb and interacted very little with me. He was going through the motions, and so was I.

Somehow, we made it through that day. I even managed to make myself eat a few bites of food, but it turned my stomach. I knew I had to take special care of the new life that was growing inside of me. I needed to eat for that child. I needed to stay strong and positive. That became my resolve. With God's grace, I began doing just that.

I still had loads of questions for God, but I didn't have time to really think about it. That was the nice thing about having so many friends and family around. Distraction! For minutes on end, I could take my mind off of my situation and think about something else. Unfortunately, that lasted for only several minutes at a time. Then, that gut-sinking pit of stabbing physical and emotional pain would return.

The next day, Tuesday, was the funeral. We had relatives drive from as far north as Canada and as far south as Texas to be there. I had cousins that I only see once a year who drove several hours to show their love and support. It was an overwhelming blessing and felt very honoring to me. That meant they took off work and school to come. They cared. They didn't need to say a word. I felt loved.

A man named Bob Ledderman, who worked with my dad, stopped briefly to express his care and concern. I hadn't been acquainted with him, though Rod knew of him. He sent someone into the hall of the church before the funeral to ask if we would come out to speak with him. He was dressed in his old work jeans and T-shirt. He said he was embarrassed and wouldn't dare come in because of the way he was dressed, but he had to stop before heading to his job. He cried with us and said he was praying for us. That was very touching and left an impression on me.

It was amazing to me to see all of the people who reached out; to see all of the people who interrupted their life for a day or a moment to show their love to us. On the other hand, there were some loved ones who couldn't make it. My Grandpa Sobota was so traumatized by Daniel's death, he decided he could not make the two-hour drive for the funeral. I was disappointed and hurt, but I tried to understand where he was with his grief. My friend Dawn wanted to be there but couldn't make it either. She lived near Baltimore and worked as a nanny. She would have had trouble getting off of work, but also didn't have the resources to travel home. It was understandable but disappointing as well.

We wanted the funeral to bring glory to God. That's how it had been planned. Yes, we talked about our precious son, Daniel. We also made sure that everyone in attendance that day wouldn't leave without hearing the hope we had through Jesus. Yes, hope we had. In the few short days since the accident, I realized that losing our child had been the worst thing I could ever imagine happening. So far, we were surviving, through the grace of God. We also somehow knew that God would carry us through it because we believed Him to be faithful, sovereign, and true. He had never let us down. Now was our chance to walk out our trust in Him. Now was our chance to let Him carry us, because we could barely put one foot in front of the other. In fact, that is more or less how we survived the next several months, one day at a time, one moment at a time, and one foot in front of the other.

The funeral did bring glory to God. If you have never experienced a true time of worship with your Savior, you are certainly missing something. When you are in a place of everything being completely out of control, the best thing you can do is throw your hands up and fall to your knees in surrender and worship. That is just what we did. We worshipped.

One song we sang echoed the hope and expectation we have of heaven. *"No more sorrow. No more pain. No more tears. No more death."* We sang that song many more times over the years. It's impossible to sing it without thinking of Daniel, what we went through those many years ago, and the absolute hope we have in heaven—a perfect place, free of pain, sadness, tears, and death.

Another song we sang was "Amazing Grace," the song Rod had sung to Daniel every night when he rocked him to sleep. Partway through the song, the sun intensified significantly and beamed through the stained-glass windows of the sanctuary. With it came an incredible sense of comfort and strength. Many people later talked about that and were noticeably impacted.

I knew God was in control. I had many, many questions for Him and hard lessons to yet learn, but I *KNEW* that God was in control and we would somehow be okay. We expressed that to Him that day as we lifted up praise to His Name! We had hope because of Jesus.

Those first three days were incredibly difficult though we were surrounded by many loved ones. We made it through that dreadful time. We still didn't understand that the worst was yet to come.

. . .

"He heals the brokenhearted and binds up their wounds" (Psalm 147:3).

"When I said, 'My foot is slipping,' your unfailing love, Lord, supported me. When anxiety was great within me, your consolation brought me joy" (Psalm 94:18-19).

"He will wipe every tear from their eyes. There will be no more death or mourning or crying or pain" (Revelation 21:4).

Chapter Five

ONE DAY AT A TIME

Rod took the rest of the week off of work. We tried to occupy our time to get our mind off of things. I honestly don't remember the details of the rest of that week. We visited my uncle Paul and aunt Judy in my hometown for a three-day getaway. I remembered pieces of that trip only after Rod stirred my memory. It was unlike our usual trips to Ohio. Typically, it was full of fun, laughter, reconnecting with many extended family members, and sharing lighthearted memories. Instead, this was a very heavy-hearted one of numbness, pain, emptiness, confusion, and many tears. It was a very difficult time. My aunt and uncle were wonderful to let us stay there and just be. We certainly weren't good company. But we needed that time away to think . . . and not think. I suppose it was therapeutic to not have to be at our home with all the fresh memories of our beautiful son. The very long minutes passed incredibly slowly that first week. I was pretty sure I couldn't continue to endure such pain and heaviness.

Some friends gave us two tickets to a Notre Dame football game. It was a wonderful gift. We would have never been able to afford such an outing. Rod had been a huge ND fan since he was a child. Being married to him, I soon followed suit. We went to the game that day, not to watch the awesome team we loved, but to try to un-feel the anguish that gripped us to the core. It didn't work. We should have felt very thrilled and caught up in the excitement of the game. We were numb. We felt nothing. We looked around us at all the rowdy people who were having a blast. It was hard to understand how they could be so carefree. Didn't they know the world as we knew it had stopped just one long week ago? Apparently not. We had to be the bearers of that reality. It was heavy.

I woke the following Monday to realize this is when everything is supposed to go back to normal. Rod returned to work. The rest of the world carried on as usual. Everyone else had gone back to work too. Everyone except me. I was home by myself. I didn't know what to do, and I was trying not to think. Thinking was too painful. When I had to think, that literally meant experiencing physical pain and that sinking feeling you sometimes get when you know something isn't right. This went on for not just days, but months and months and months.

I walked around the house mostly numb. I was still in shock that this was my reality. I was supposed to go on like normal, but life would never be normal again. Life was forever changed. I had to find a new normal. But how? I picked up toys and I cried. I did laundry and I cried as I folded little outfits for the last time. I even held blankets to smell them, and, of course, I cried more tears. I looked at the fingerprints on the windows and full-length mirror and decided they would stay. I didn't want to be alone, but I didn't have the physical or emotional strength to talk to anyone. What was I doing? Who was I? What was I supposed to do? What was my purpose?

I had many chats with God in the following days and weeks. There were times I shouted at Him. I like to think of it like I shouted "to" Him. After all, I needed to vent to someone. I knew He could handle that. "It isn't fair!" And it really wasn't fair. For anyone who has gone through a difficult or devastating time, you know it's not fair! You're so right. One thing that helped bring understanding was knowing that Jesus died for me. He paid for all of my (and your) sins when He died a cruel and ugly death on the cross. I can stand before God with a clean slate because of the price Jesus paid for me! That's not fair. But I love it. It's so true that life is not fair, but it goes both ways. So, I choose to accept it.

It comforts me to know that even Jesus asked God a question, seemingly not understanding His divine plan or will for the situation. As Jesus hung on the cross in agony, He cried in a loud voice, "'My God, my God, why have you forsaken me?'" (Matthew 27:46b). Jesus knew His Father was faithful and sovereign, yet He uttered those words. That's how I know it is okay to ask God questions and voice our concerns to Him. We know through scripture that God never leaves us or forsakes us, though sometimes it may feel like He does.

Though I had a few emotional shouting sessions with God, I felt love for Him, and deep down I trusted Him. Even so, it didn't negate my emotions, confusion, and need for deep healing. I sensed that He would answer my questions in time because it was too much for me then. It just didn't make sense. Nevertheless, I trusted God. He was all I really had. All I really knew was that He is faithful and true. I had to hold on to that. I had already made up my mind to continue serving Him wholeheartedly with everything I had.

I knew I had to keep a strong, positive attitude for my new baby. It was my goal, and it became my new purpose. After all, my main purpose in life had been to be a stay-at-home mom and raise my children in the best way that I could. What was I supposed to do now? I had no child to care for. I was no longer a mom. Who was I? My identity was shaken. It made me feel stripped and vulnerable. In a strange way, I even felt guilty for not contributing something to the world around me. I simply didn't know what to do or who to be. I was in no state of mind to be of help to anyone anyway.

* * *

During the week after Daniel died, I sat down one morning at the table with my coffee and my Bible. Somehow I ended up in the book of James and began reading.

"Consider it pure joy . . . whenever you face trials of many kinds" (James 1:2). I stared at the pages. It made no sense. Consider it *joy* when you face trials? Really? I didn't understand. At all. So I prayed. *"Lord, I want to trust You, and I want to understand all of this, but I don't. I really need You to help this make sense to me. Please, help me. I am desperate to understand."* I looked back at the pages and stared numbly at them. Just then, in the background, I could faintly hear the radio. It was Dr. David Jeremiah, from *Turning Point*, broadcasting from WFRN, our local Christian radio station out of Elkhart, Indiana. He said, ". . . And today we are going to focus on the book of James, chapter one." I couldn't believe my ears. I turned up the radio and sat back while God brought His *rhema* word right to me. (*Rhema* means a personal word from God.) When the half-hour broadcast was over, I understood James chapter one, and I understood a little more of the heart of God. What an exciting turning point for me! (I never realized until I penned those words that the title of that broadcast was very fitting. It *was* a turning point.)

I began understanding how a person could have joy when she doesn't have happiness. With God, that is possible. So I focused on the contentment I had in my Jesus. I tried to overlook the lack of true happiness, because, after all, it was nowhere to be found.

I also realized that the scripture says *when* you go through various trials. . . . It doesn't say "if," but "when." That brought a measure of peace to my heart; being more settled in the idea that we didn't deserve what happened, but beginning to understand that trials *will come*. That is one example of different ways we learned and grew from our situation.

I struggled with not knowing how I could love another child like I loved my Daniel. I know that is every mother's question when she is expecting child number two. It's natural to not understand how that love can be shared. I would later understand and experience loving another child in the same way.

The spotting I had in the beginning of my pregnancy stopped. If I remember correctly, it had even stopped before the funeral. I knew I wouldn't lose the baby. We had an ultrasound to confirm everything was okay, and we learned we were expecting another boy. Rod was thrilled. His paternal grandfather had only one son, Randy, who is Rod's father. Randy had only one son, Rod. Rod had wondered with great distress if we would ever have another son to carry on the family name. He was almost in disbelief when he learned we would indeed have another boy.

I didn't know how I could possibly love this child as much as Daniel. In spite of that, I maintained a positive attitude. That was a good thing, because Rod struggled to have one.

Rod was miserable every day, more so than me. He didn't want to talk about the accident and couldn't handle hearing memories about our son. Any kind of happy memory would somehow turn around and take him right back to the accident. So we didn't talk about Daniel. That was the most difficult thing for me. I needed to talk about him and remember. Thank God I had friends and relatives I could talk to. I learned that when someone loses a loved one, you shouldn't avoid talking about them to prevent pain. On the contrary, it is quite healing to reminisce. I would occasionally open the photo album and remember—and cry. They were healing tears. I think all tears are tears of healing. I think a very important part of dealing with grief is facing the emotions, and sometimes that means allowing yourself to cry.

Those first few weeks and months were definitely the hardest part. The quiet house was agonizing. Finding a random toy behind a chair would take my breath away. I had many lonely crying sessions. The reality began to set in. We learned the hard way that when the funeral is over and you try to find a new normal, that is the difficult part. When the loved one of someone you know passes away, make sure you are there for them *after* the funeral. Of course, everyone grieves differently. The people who reached out to me then are what helped me keep my sanity. I needed someone to talk to. I loved it when people shared memories or stories of Daniel. It brought such delight to my heart. For moments, I could forget about that gut-wrenching pain in the pit of my stomach. It was still there, every day.

I now know that Rod was probably experiencing Post Traumatic Stress Disorder (PTSD). His responses and withdrawal weren't just his way of grieving; they were his way of surviving. Maybe this could explain the actions or the emotional absence of someone you know. Help them to press through it and get in touch with the grieving process. It's a very real and lonely thing people go through. Try to be a support. (See Appendix B for more information on PTSD.)

. . .

There were times when we spoke to others who had lost a child. That actually brought a sense of sanity to my floundering mind. While I didn't like being part of "the club," I did find it very helpful to know others had literally survived losing a child. It gave me hope that I too could survive. During the first month or so after the accident, I had truly wondered if I could.

I spoke to my mother-in-law's cousin Ruth Coblentz, who had lost not one, but *three* children at various ages. I sincerely didn't know how anyone could live through that and be in their right mind. She gave me hope upon hope that I could come through it and be whole again. My phone conversation with her was so very valuable just two weeks after Daniel passed. Her words were a lifeline to me.

. . .

I needed something to fill my days so I didn't go stir crazy. The people who used to stop by occasionally no longer dropped in. I was lonely. I had too much idle time on my hands. Rod's aunt Ramona King encouraged me to consider volunteering at a local day care which she ran. I decided that would be a good idea. It certainly helped take my mind off of myself, but it was too much for me. Watching other people's children grow and smile and make people laugh was too difficult. Holding babies that weren't mine reminded me of how "robbed" I felt. It was near torture when the parents arrived at the end of their work shift to pick up their children. They got to hug them, kiss them, hear about the fun parts of the day, and take them home. When the children were gone, I went home . . . by myself. After a month, I knew I had to do something different. Everyone understood.

I began volunteering in my church office. What a godsend that was! Not only could I get my mind off of myself and my pain for a while, but I had other wonderful people around me that could speak life and encouragement into me. Pastor Vic and I had several chats during those months that helped me process things differently and moved me steps closer to healing. I appreciated him doing that, considering he had a busy schedule. That meant a lot to me. Also, Pastor Ross let me talk and process my feelings and helped me to see that I was normal, my thoughts were normal, my questions were normal, and things would continue getting better. That kind of support felt lifesaving to me and gave me so much hope.

I don't know that I was much help in the church office. I have to laugh because I wasn't very fast at typing. I wasn't very fast at anything. I made plenty of mistakes. I justified it all to myself, knowing that at least they weren't paying me. I was just volunteering, so they'd have to live with my slow, unskilled self. I did that for about six months, and I grew exponentially. (I'm not referring to my belly, though that grew too.) I learned so much about the gifts God had placed in me, skills that I hadn't even begun to tap into. Things like serving (which is another way to say giving my time to bless others), organizing, creativity, encouragement, and a knack for seeing details that needed to be taken care of. It's different when you naturally use your gifts or skills in your own home. When you use them to bless others, you begin to see the potential and purpose you were created for. I began having a purpose again. It felt wonderful. I was creating a new normal, and I liked it.

. . .

"For it is God who works in you to will and to act in order to fulfill his good purposes" (Philippians 2:13).

"Many are the plans in a person's heart, but it is the Lord's purpose that prevails" (Proverbs 19:21).

"Though the fig tree does not bud and there are no grapes on the vines, though the olive crop fails and the fields produce no food, though there are no sheep in the pen and no cattle in the stalls, yet I will rejoice in the Lord, I will be joyful in God my Savior" (Habakkuk 3:17-18).

Chapter Six

SURVIVING THE FIRST YEAR

I was expecting Christopher in April 1995. When March rolled around, I knew I had to sort through all of Daniel's clothes that were still in the drawers and put newborn baby clothes in them. I had dreaded that day. I felt as though I couldn't put it off any longer, so I finally tackled that project. With every outfit I pulled out of the drawer came a flood of memories from when Daniel wore it. It was an incredibly difficult, emotional day, but I'm sure very healing at the same time. I bawled for hours as I sorted clothes. I remember gasping for air at times as the sobs put a choke hold on me. I had to stop to catch my breath; the tears and emotions came that forcefully. In a sense, I had been denying my true emotions in order to stay positive for the baby I would meet in one short month. That day, it was utterly impossible to be strong and positive. Finally, my chore was done, and the baby clothes were in the drawers. I packed Daniel's clothes in a box and put them in a closet. It felt like I was pushing forward to the next chapter, whatever that meant.

Since I was moving forward in a fresh direction, I also decided it was time to wash my mirror and windows. That meant wash those little fingerprints off. It was time.

I had dinner ready as usual when Rod arrived home from work. I was so pleased that I had gotten a great deal done that day. As Rod came up the stairs that evening, he looked curiously at the full-length mirror that hung on our bedroom door. He got closer to inspect the mirror and immediately became angry. To my surprise, he noticed the fingerprints were gone. I had no idea he looked at those every day upon arriving home. He was quite taken aback by my cleaning feat and immediately became heavy-hearted and depressed for the rest of the evening. Once again, he didn't want to talk about anything because it hurt too much. I had to have grace for his response, because that's where he was in his stages of grief. I grieved my *mistake* of washing the mirror and windows without thinking about him. My accomplished day of pushing past difficult tasks became just another struggle that tried to wedge its way into our marriage.

. . .

Christopher John Chupp was born by another unplanned C-section on April 25, 1995. He was born at 11:58 p.m. If he would have arrived two minutes later, he would have been born on his actual due date.

I was a mess. During the delivery, which I was awake for, I saw the doctor lift up a somewhat dusky blue infant. He wasn't breathing. I immediately thought he was dead, and without consciously thinking about it, I willed myself to not get attached to him. I could never handle loving and losing another child. I wasn't thinking about the fact that he was born C-section, and that that is somewhat normal until the baby is suctioned orally and stimulated. Within a minute, he was crying and breathing normally. His color turned to a desired shade of pink, but it was too late. Somehow, my emotions couldn't connect with him. He was just there. I was incredibly disappointed that I had failed *again* as a mom and couldn't deliver him naturally. I have since worked through that false sense of failure and guilt, but at the time it was a huge defeat to me mentally. It was another way that God didn't come through for me the way I wanted Him to. I was immediately depressed! I had stayed strong for Chris while I carried him. At that point, I seemingly let my guard down. I no longer had the strength to choose or pretend to be positive. I became aware of my raw pain, but in a sense I couldn't feel anything, especially a bond with him. My life felt like such a failure at every turn. It was difficult to even hope.

I struggled with rejection from Rod, who went to work while I lay in the hospital recovering and trying to muster up a connection with my child. That wasn't how it was supposed to be. It was supposed to be a happy moment. But it wasn't. It was a very difficult time.

I felt bad for anyone who visited me during those three days. Honestly, it was a blur. I looked terrible because I didn't care about anything, especially me. I wasn't taking care of myself. I was emotionless. I was barely taking care of my baby. I would nurse him, then give him to the nurses. It was too much for me. I remember a friend stopping by for a visit and attempting to cheer me up. I couldn't muster up the emotional strength to even pretend I was happy to see Sherry—not because of her, but because of me. I was a mess in every sense. I knew it, yet I didn't have the energy to do anything about it. I wanted her to leave so I didn't have to entertain her or answer her questions about how things were going. Things weren't going well, and, frankly, I didn't want to have to explain that. I wanted to make everything be the way it was supposed to be, but that was impossible. I was in survival mode. The truth was it was all I could do to not burst into tears, let alone put on a smile and a façade. She saw a very dark side of my emotional state that day. Looking back, she was so gracious and encouraging to me. I could tell by the look in her eyes that she wanted to scoop me up in her arms, comfort me, and make everything better. She could probably tell by the look in my eyes that it was best for her to keep her distance. I was more than fine with that.

The next day, after nursing Chris, the nurse came to get him and informed me they were taking him to the nurse's station for a scheduled procedure. I was told that I could go, too, but I didn't care to. About five or ten minutes later, I heard a baby wailing. I assumed it was *my* baby, and my mother's heart leapt. All I knew at that moment was that I needed to go comfort my baby. That was the beginning of our bonding.

Slowly over the next month, God brought a healing to my wounded heart, and I felt a total connection with Chris. It was a miracle in my eyes, and I praise God for that. I suspect post-partum blues had also been a factor, yet that too began to pass. We were back on the road to normalcy. Chris brought a type of joy back into our empty home that gave Rod and I something to talk about and be proud of. Our marriage relationship definitely had its struggles. Having a baby back in our home was a wonderful reprieve to the previous eight months of silent grieving.

Having a baby didn't fix everything or stop our feelings of grief. When you lose a loved one, there is a void that is very challenging to fill. It takes years to work through it completely. Having Chris definitely added an aspect of joy, contentment, and even hope into our lives—hope to be truly happy again. We were beginning to make progress, though it was only through baby steps.

. . .

On July 18, we chose to celebrate Daniel's birthday with a cake. We watched old home videos of him and looked through our photo album. We decided to make his birthday a positive occasion rather than a depressing event. There's no doubt it was difficult. We had many tears, but we also laughed. We laughed at our funny, energetic, happy little boy that we knew we would see again someday. (We have made that a tradition every year.)

. . .

When Labor Day weekend rolled around, we couldn't bear the thought of being home. We wanted to get away so we weren't faced with countless questions of how we were doing. We were surviving. We weren't doing great, but we were surviving. I continued to purpose to stay positive. It was my goal to let God be glorified in our lives and in the way He was bringing healing to us.

Rod continued to not talk about anything of real importance. As long as a conversation was on a surface level, he was fine. If I mentioned Daniel or the anniversary of his death, Rod would simply shut down. He would withdraw and shut me out. Because he was struggling, I felt I had to be strong. That's how marriage works: You balance each other out. You fill in the gaps for each other.

We decided to go to Baltimore, Maryland, to visit Dawn. It ended up being a significant turning point for us. We arrived very late on the Friday night of Labor Day weekend. I woke late on Saturday morning. That very day, one year earlier, my firstborn son had gone to be with Jesus. The nagging, pulling pain in my inner core was still fresh every time I thought about it. Those thoughts were less and less frequent, thank God, but the pang it left me with was just as strong as a year earlier. I hated that and wondered when or if that would ever go away.

I couldn't bring myself to get out of bed and face anyone that morning. Rod had been up and long gone as was his usual routine. He has always been an early riser. He must have taken four-month-old Chris with him. I was happy he did. I turned the radio on and searched for a Christian station so I could find encouragement to give me strength to face the day. I found a station and began listening to the uplifting music. That too quickly ended when a man began sharing a message. *"Oh great! Just what I wanted,"* I sarcastically thought. I lay in bed, unable to get up, unable to switch the channel, so I listened. I don't remember the exact message I heard that day, yet I do know that it caused me to break. The speaker (who was speaking right to me) challenged his listeners to quit holding up a façade. He challenged me to be real with what I was feeling. He encouraged me to quit leaning on my own strength and instead turn to Jesus for His never-ending strength. I have a habit of being self-sufficient and taking care of what needs to be done. Sometimes, I need a reminder that my strength has to come from my Jesus. In that moment, it hit me that I hadn't really let Jesus help me walk it out. I had been trying to live through grief by just surviving. I knew I was exhausted and couldn't do it anymore. My physical body and my emotional being felt as weak as ever. I draped myself over the bed, and I broke. I sobbed tears from a deep, deep place within that I had been holding back for much of that year in order to be strong. I had cried many tears during that first year, yet it seemed, for the first time, I bore all of my pain. I let it unravel. I allowed myself to be very vulnerable and real with God and my feelings that day. These were tears that came from a depth that I had to allow God to expose in order to bring healing, a depth I wasn't aware of. I was raw and wounded. It was just me and God. I laid there almost in a state of oblivion to the world around me. I was so wounded, and I was finally able to admit it.

A short time later, something miraculous happened. Rod came in the room. My first thought was, "I have to pull myself together so I don't upset him," but I couldn't. I continued to sob. I didn't want him to look at me. I didn't want to have to deal with his melancholy mood. He came to me to find out what was wrong. I tried to explain. Then, he told me he had just come to tell me what God was revealing to him. He explained that God had removed the blinders from his eyes, which allowed him to realize how self-focused he'd been while trying to work through his grief. He had had a true revelation and healing from God. I saw light in his eyes for the first time in one solid year. I could tell he was different. Just like that, God did a work in his heart and mind. And just like that, Rod and I switched places in our grief. I became weak, and he became strong. That is the most tangible demonstration I've ever known of spouses supporting and being a helpmate to one another. It felt just like the way marriage should work. When one is down, the other is there to pick him up, and vice versa. Even though it was the beginning of a whole new level of grief for me, I saw God come through in a miraculous way. Once again, God confirmed to me that He is faithful and sovereign, a God of miracles and of healing.

We discovered Chris's first tooth that morning. It was a day of breakthrough.

. . .

"You will know the truth, and the truth will set you free" (John 8:32).

"See, I am doing a new thing! Now it springs up; do you not perceive it? I am making a way in the wilderness and streams in the wasteland" (Isaiah 43:19).

"Now to him who is able to do immeasurably more than all we ask or imagine, according to his power that is at work within us, to him be glory in the church and in Christ Jesus throughout all generations, for ever and ever! Amen" (Ephesians 3:20-21).

Chapter Seven

HOPING TO HOPE

In the first year or two after the accident, there were many times when I would see someone I hadn't seen since before the accident. I could be going about a normal day, feeling pretty good, when suddenly someone would come around a corner at the grocery store. Our eyes would meet. Initially, I would be happy to see my friend or relative. Inevitably, their eyes would darken. Their smile would turn down. The all-too-common look of pity or sadness would present itself. Then, like an inward spiral punching me in the gut, I would realize what was happening. Because they hadn't seen me or Rod since the accident, they were now reliving their sorrow toward us. At that point, no matter where I was with my emotions, I would instantly be brought back to remembrance and sadness. That was difficult for Rod and me both. It is a normal thing that people experience; nonetheless, it was tough. A happy-go-lucky moment in the day could instantly turn to a stone-cold revisitation of our saddest day. Sigh!

Now, you may think you should not approach people this way to give your condolences and share your concern. On the contrary, please do show your friends and community members that you care. It will definitely take them back to that remembrance of sadness, but it will be worth it down the road. They will learn that that part of the grieving process is common. It really does mean a lot to know how much people remember, care, and want to help in whatever way they can. The truth of the matter is, other than prayer and being there for emotional support or a sounding board, there is not a lot others can actually *do*. So go ahead and reach out to those friends and loved ones you care so much about. They will mostly remember that you cared.

* * *

The second year after the accident was difficult for me, but necessary for my healing. Rod continued to be positive and encouraging. He allowed me to continue to grieve the way I needed to just as I had done for him. Our marriage was growing stronger. We were finding more and more happiness in the everyday things of life. We had definitely settled on a new normal, and it was beginning to feel good again.

I was asked to share at a ladies' event at our church. I had never in my life wanted to get up in front of a group of people and talk. I would have done anything to avoid that. I'm a behind-the-scenes kind of person. When I was in high school, I would willingly take a lower grade in my literature classes to avoid having to answer a question in front of the class. I was incredibly insecure. However, God had given me an impression that I would be speaking in front of a group of women. It resonated with my heart, so I agreed to take the challenge and do my first public speaking engagement. It wouldn't be my last.

I shared pieces of my testimony, my story. I talked about the accident and about the amazing things God had been up to. I gave God the glory, which I always come back to, because without Him, I have little to offer. I am whole through Him. I am a different person today with Jesus Christ in my life than I was as an insecure teenager who thought she had nothing to offer the world. I have a lot to offer the world. Not because I'm so talented—I'm actually not. But because I submit my heart and life to Christ, He fills in the gaps. He takes my tests and turns them into my testimony. He takes my messes and turns them into my message. In 1995, I began my speaking, teaching, encouraging, and mentoring ministry to women. It has been a passion of my heart since. God gave me the confidence and boldness to say yes. He works through me (another miracle) to communicate His message to the hearts of other women.

God wants people to understand they have a calling and a purpose, they are valuable in His eyes, and He loves them no matter what. He wants them to have hope and to trust Him. I love being a part of sharing those truths with people. It's an exhilarating feeling to watch someone have those truths click in their mind and resonate in their heart. It's amazing to watch people's eyes be opened to the amazing and healing truths of God. To watch people find a sense of belonging and worth is priceless. That's the passion God has placed in my heart. It all began the first time I took that step of boldness to share publicly. (I was shaking in my shoes!)

I have to ask you, what is it that God has placed on your heart, but fear has caused you to hold back? Do you know what is on the other side of that fear? It's freedom—freedom to walk out the calling and purpose for which God has created you. Don't let that be stolen from you because of fear. Push through, overcome that fear, and watch how you come out on the other side. It will blow your mind. It did mine. Remember this verse: "The one who calls you is faithful, and he will do it" (I Thessalonians 5:24).

I continued to volunteer in the church and other places in various ways and continued to let God guide me every day. That's where peace comes in. It doesn't matter if you accomplish little or much in your day. It doesn't matter if you feel like you have found your calling or not. The bottom line is, are you seeking and following God daily? When you do, you will have peace and fulfillment. After two years, the gut-wrenching pain slowly turned into a tickle, similar to when you get butterflies in your stomach. God was continually bringing healing to me. I believe it had a lot to do with me cooperating with that healing process.

People say time heals. There is some truth in that, but time itself doesn't heal; it just helps. Healing comes when you face your grief. I can't imagine facing that grief without the hope of God. I know I will see my baby boy again someday. I know because I have the hope and confidence that he is in heaven with Jesus. That brings me great comfort and joy.

. . .

"'My grace is sufficient for you, for my power is made perfect in weakness.' Therefore I will boast all the more gladly about my weaknesses, so that Christ's power may rest on me. That is why, for Christ's sake, I delight in weaknesses, in insults, in hardships, in persecutions, in difficulties. For when I am weak, then I am strong" (2 Corinthians 12:9-10).

"We are hard pressed on every side, but not crushed; perplexed, but not in despair; persecuted, but not abandoned; struck down, but not destroyed" (2 Corinthians 4:8-9).

"Praise be to the God and Father of our Lord Jesus Christ, the Father of compassion and the God of all comfort, who comforts us in all our troubles, so that we can comfort those in any trouble with the comfort we ourselves receive from God" (2 Corinthians 1:3-4).

Chapter Eight

A LIGHTER HEART

Life seemed to be back on track. Chris was about eighteen months old and was quite a strong-willed little guy. I was at home one afternoon, and something happened that I'd never experienced before. Out of the blue, I had a vision (I had not been praying or seeking God). It was just like a dream, but it was in broad daylight while I was awake. I saw myself walking into our nursery with a small baby in my arms, and somehow I knew it was a girl. I actually blinked my eyes several times and looked around. It was gone. I had had a vision, and I knew it was from God. At that point, I had not wanted to plan for more children. I was still on a healing journey and felt like my hands were full, but that vision put a spark in my heart and caused me to be open to having another child.

I discovered less than a month later that I was expecting. I knew it would be a girl. I even carried her differently than I did the boys. I did not have an ultrasound, so we didn't know for sure during the whole pregnancy. But I knew. Rebecca Erin Chupp was delivered by a scheduled C-section on August 14, 1997. I was so delighted to have a girl. Again, having had local anesthesia, I was able to be awake for delivery. I knew better what to expect this time. She was born on a good friend's birthday, which helped to solve the name dilemma. We named her after our good friend Becky, although we call our daughter Becca.

Becca was an easy baby. She slept through the night after just a few short months. That was quite different from what we had experienced with both boys.

In many ways, I was becoming like my old self again, although I don't believe I ever got back that part of me that didn't *know* what tragedy was. Before Daniel died, I was somewhat naïve and perhaps even clueless in some regards to grief. I would go so far as to say I had a Pollyanna-type view of Christianity. *If you live right, good things happen and you receive blessings. If you don't live right, you open yourself up to trouble and heartache.* That is a nice idea, I suppose, but it is simply not true. Bad, and sometimes horrible, things happen to good people. That's one thing I had a difficult time wrapping my mind around. Over time, I accepted it, though it's a difficult concept to truly grasp.

God is a God of love and mercy. He is a fair and just God. He is faithful and sovereign. He loves us so much that He created us with a free will. That means we get to choose whether we will love and serve Him or not. He loves us so much that He would never force us to serve Him. It's a beautiful thing.

Because people have a free will, we sometimes don't make good choices. Sometimes the poor choices people make hurt others. We wonder why God allows some things to happen when it causes harm to someone else. It comes back to the fact that He will never force Himself on us. He will never take away our free will and our choice. So, unfortunately, bad things do happen in the world we live in, often as a result of someone's poor choice. Accidents happen. But the redeeming truth is that heaven will be perfect! Those who love Him and choose freely to live for Him will have a home in heaven. Let me demonstrate that with a few scriptures.

"For God so loved the world that he gave his one and only Son, that whoever believes in him shall not perish but have eternal life" (John 3:16).

"For all have sinned and fall short of the glory of God, and are justified freely by his grace through the redemption that came by Christ Jesus" (Romans 3:23-24).

"But God demonstrates his own love for us in this: While we were still sinners, Christ died for us" (Romans 5:8).

"If you declare with your mouth, 'Jesus is Lord,' and believe in your heart that God raised him from the dead, you will be saved" (Romans 10:9).

Reading those scriptures is so exciting and life-giving to me. They are so full of hope and grace. Jesus made a way for us, and all we have to do is accept Him. Salvation is a free gift. It's a very complex thing that God made very simple. Choose Him. It is a life-changing decision!

The Christian walk is all about grace, hope, and life. We *will* have trials and hardships. Remember that scripture in James 1:2? *When* we go through trials of various kinds . . . Not "if," but "when." Trials are bound to happen. But when we have Jesus in our life to lead us, guide us, and show us His truth, we know that even our tragedies can turn around because of hope. He is a God of redemption.

Jesus tells us in John 10:10 that He came to give us life more abundantly. Don't get stuck in a pit of despair after a trial or tragedy in your life. Look to Jesus with hope. "And we know that in all things God works for the good of those who love him, who have been called according to his purpose" (Romans 8:28). ALL things! If you are walking with Jesus, you can bank on that promise. He says in Jeremiah 31:13b, "I will turn their mourning into gladness; I will give them comfort and joy instead of sorrow." I hope these scriptures are bringing you encouragement. They are to me! These are promises of God. These scriptures and many others are what comforted me and gave me hope in the months and years after our son died.

We all have the opportunity to grow through difficult circumstances. I did. I grew up. I learned and understood more of the reality of life. I didn't like it. But I did grow to learn there was nothing I could do to change it.

One day, well into the third year after Daniel died, I realized that the ache in the pit of my stomach was no longer a daily part of me. Until that point, every time I thought of him or the accident, I had physical symptoms of pain. It did ease up over the years. It wasn't nearly as bad the second year. It was even better that third year. Now, it was finally gone. I rejoiced! I cried. I thanked and praised God for His continued healing in my life. At that point, my life was not what it should have been, but it was good. I had found a new "normal."

◦ ◦ ◦

"*Come near to God and he will come near to you*" (James 4:8a).

"*For his anger lasts only a moment, but his favor lasts a lifetime; weeping may remain for a night, but rejoicing comes in the morning*" (Psalm 30:5).

"*Those who sow in tears will reap with songs of joy*" (Psalm 126:5).

Chapter Nine

THE CONTINUUM
OF HEALING

Five years after the accident, life felt full with a two- and four-year-old. My life as a stay-at-home mom of two children was busy and sometimes chaotic. I continued to serve through our church in a number of ways. I sometimes met with other moms for play dates with our children. Make no mistake, it was really a play date for us moms. We enjoyed coffee gatherings and sometimes planned for lunch too. Everything we did together was on a tight budget. We found ways to spend time together and encourage one another. Thank God for friends.

Once again, God put a thought in my head about having another child. I didn't know if I could handle that very well. But I decided to not rule it out. I continued to move further toward emotional healing. For those who are unfamiliar with the death of someone very close, I need to tell you something. Yes, it can take *that long* for healing to happen. And that is normal. The death of a close loved one, especially a child, is such a permanently life-altering event. Unless you experience it (and I pray you never do), you can't possibly understand the depth of devastation that happens. You can care, you can love, you can empathize, you can try to understand, but unless you go through that life-changing event, there is no way you can possibly understand the deprivation you experience with a loss like that.

I hope to paint a picture of the reality of what people go through when they lose a child. I'd love to tell you after a few months you get back on track, choose a positive attitude, and move forward. Unfortunately, I can't tell you that. The anguish that occurs takes a long, long time to truly heal. You must choose to press forward in your healing process, or it could take much longer. In fact, if you choose (consciously or subconsciously) to live in the self-pity or denial stage, you may never find that place of true healing. Healing is a process. Again, I will agree that time does help with that process, but time itself does not heal. God does.

Emotional healing is similar to the healing of a physical wound. A cut or burn takes time to heal. It hurts until it is healed. As the healing progresses, the pain turns to an ache, then to tenderness. The pain we have while a wound is healing is to remind us to be careful and give extra care to that area. Time helps a wound heal, but if there is something in the wound that irritates it, it will not heal properly. I hope this helps you understand why the healing of emotional pain also takes time. If we let bitterness or anger take root in our emotional wound, healing cannot fully occur. It is impossible. It's important in many situations to also walk through the process of forgiveness in order to move forward in healing. Don't let those negative things hold you back from true healing and joy. Give your emotional wounds time to heal.

I love to remember these verses:

Do not be anxious about anything, but in everything, by prayer and petition, with thanksgiving, present your requests to God. And the peace of God, which transcends all understanding, will guard your hearts and your minds in Christ Jesus.

Finally, brothers, whatever is true, whatever is noble, whatever is right, whatever is pure, whatever is lovely, whatever is admirable— if anything is excellent or praiseworthy—think about such things.
(Philippians 4:6-8)

We should give thanks *in* everything. That means, in spite of our circumstances, we know that God has a bigger plan, one that we likely don't understand. He will work all things together for good. For that, we can give thanks.

Do you want to know the keys to healing? I believe the keys are to allow yourself to grieve, give God your daily struggles with grief, allow Him to bring peace to your heart, and dwell on good things. I don't ever want you to feel like you need to be in denial of your pain in order to focus on positive things. No! Allow yourself to feel pain. Cry. Grieve. Then, turn your thoughts to the hope you have in Jesus. Don't stay in that painful place in your mind too long. It will eat you up. Allow time in your day for grief, but also choose times to focus on brighter things. Don't be afraid to smile and laugh. It is so important to give yourself permission to do that. It's okay. And it actually helps push you toward healing.

Rod remembers the first time that he was feeling happy after the accident. He was enjoying himself for the first time in months. When he realized his joyful, carefree emotions, it caught him off guard. He instantly felt guilt.

Initially, he made a choice to stop being happy and remember his grief. Don't do that! Allow yourself fully to experience moments of joy. It can be lifesaving.

Later that year on December 29, 1999, we were blessed with our third baby boy, Justus Alexander Chupp. It was my fourth, and would be my last, C-section. I do have to say, recovery from a planned C-section is so much easier than going through full labor *and* a C-section. Unfortunately, that time I ended up with a spinal headache for five days. It was only somewhat tolerable if I lay flat. When I had to sit up for any reason, the pain was excruciating. It honestly felt worse than labor. I brought in the new millennium in the hospital, feeling awful.

Going home with a newborn and two other children (four and under) and having a spinal headache wasn't fun, to say the least. It was not fun at all. Fortunately, I had some of Rod's young cousins volunteer to help keep the older kids occupied while he was at work. They brought Justus to me when he was hungry. They even changed his diapers. They would entertain Chris and Becca and help them with their daily needs. It would have been impossible for me to have made it through those first three days home without Daniel, Anna, and Katherine.

Honestly, those first days and weeks were a blur. It took me nearly two months to adjust to having three children. The variety of needs was daunting to me. I eventually got a routine down and everything became normal. Well, as normal as life can be with three small children and their ever-changing needs.

I continued to heal.

. . .

"Then he said to her, 'Daughter, your faith has healed you. Go in peace'" (Luke 8:48).

"Praise the lord, my soul, and forget not all his benefits—who forgives all your sins and heals all your diseases, who redeems your life from the pit and crowns you with love and compassion, who satisfies your desires with good things so that your youth is renewed like the eagle's" (Psalm 103:2-5).

"Lord my God, I called to you for help, and you healed me" (Psalm 30:2).

Chapter Ten

THE SEVEN-YEAR BLESSING

♥ Seven years after the accident, I was doing life with my man, six-year-old Chris, four-year-old Becca, and almost-two-year-old Justus. Life was good. It was a very busy time in my life, but I look back on it as some of the fondest years. As overwhelming as my days often felt, it was also such a sweet time with the kids. They had long days of play time together. We made time for fun excursions in between the daily household tasks. I was into my eighth year of using and washing cloth diapers, and so ready to be out of that stage. Great memories, that's what those years held for me.

Justus, Becca and Chris in 2002

Family photo October 2002

Near that seven-year mark, I had a realization. A wonderful realization! I felt like God had completed a healing work in my heart regarding Daniel's death. I will try to explain. The grief wasn't there like it had been. When I thought of my sweet Daniel, I could think of the precious memories, and I would be sad to no longer have him in my life, but the daily grief was gone. When I came to that realization one day, I literally danced for joy in my living room and cried tears of thanksgiving. What a day to remember that was! I knew God was faithful and sovereign. That day, I felt it to the core of my being. He truly is a God of healing and redemption. I had a feeling of victory!

I look back at something I considered the most difficult thing I could ever think of happening: losing a child. It happened, and I have to reflect on the faithfulness of my Lord. He not only walked me through it, but I was victorious! I knew that if I could make it through that, He would walk me through anything. He has.

• • •

I have heard and been taught that the number seven is a number of wholeness and completion. In light of that, I think it is so interesting that it was at the seven-year mark that I felt God's fullness of healing in my life. Let me be sure to communicate that everyone's healing journey is different. If your healing takes five years or ten years, that is okay. You need to walk through your grief and press into your healing at the rate God takes you through it. There is no magic number. For those of you watching someone grieve and wishing they would hurry up, please reconsider. Instead, encourage them in biblical truth, walk with them through the grieving process, give them space when needed, and pray for God to bring revelation to their heart and mind so they can move forward. There's never a "normal" amount of time for grieving. Nor is there a normal way to grieve.

. . .

As I reflected, I realized that during those seven long years I learned a lot about what to do, or not do, when someone loses a child (or anyone for that matter). The best way to show love and support is to be there at the visitation or the funeral, or even stop by their house sometime in the first few weeks or months. You don't have to say a word. Your gift of time or a hug says all you need to say. If you feel uncomfortable and don't know what to say, don't say much. You can say, "I'm sorry," and, "I'm praying for you." That's enough. Sometimes, in the stress of feeling like we have to say something profound or meaningful, we end up saying something that may not sound or feel very comforting.

If a child dies, it doesn't mean God needed another flower for His flower garden. He didn't need another angel. It doesn't help to say, "Well, at least you can have more children." My child didn't die because God knew I was strong enough to handle it.

God will walk with *anyone* through the loss of a child. He will never leave us or forsake us. His strength is made perfect in our weakness. We can do *all things* through Christ who gives us strength. Those are truths of His word. Let them become a reality to you. (These scriptures can be found in Deuteronomy 31:6, 2 Corinthians 12:9, and Philippians 4:13.)

If you have prayed and prayed for something to turn around in your life but it doesn't, don't bear the burden that it is your fault. Sometime we, or others, think we didn't have enough faith. The Bible explains that if we have the faith of a mustard seed, we can move mountains. That confirms to me that even the smallest amount of faith and trust in God can change our circumstances. So if our prayers don't get answered the way we want them to, yet we have faith, we can know that God has allowed something and has a bigger or different plan in mind. He doesn't always give us what we want, but He does give us what we need. He wants to use our "unanswered" prayer to work together for a greater good in our life. His ways are higher than our ways. His thoughts are higher than our thoughts (Isaiah 55:9).

God always answers our prayers. Unfortunately, it may not be the answer we are hoping for. His answer can be "Yes," "No," "Maybe" (depending on some specific things), or "Wait." If you prayed something fervently but didn't receive the specific answer you had prayed for, don't feel like God abandoned you and didn't answer your prayer.

For those of you with children, imagine with me a few pleas your child might bring to you. "Can I have a cookie?" Well, if it's just before dinner time, you will likely tell your child to wait. Does that mean you don't love your child? Of course not. It means you are looking ahead and know it would be better for that child to wait until after dinner. If he asks, "Can I go play basketball on the street since my ball won't bounce on the grass in the yard?" You will most likely say, "No." Your answer is no because you care deeply for your child and don't want him to potentially get hurt by a passing car. He will probably not understand that. Can you see how God might answer with "No" or "Wait" and have a bigger picture in mind? A bigger picture that we may or may not understand down the road.

That September day in 1994, God most definitely did not answer the prayers that Rod and I had in the way we wanted Him to answer. Nonetheless, He certainly worked all things together for good. I have learned so much about God and His ways. I have grown so much spiritually. Rod and I have ministered to dozens of families who have lost a child. We have been able to speak life and hope into situations that felt hopeless. Knowing all that, would I lose him all over again? *NEVER!* Never would anyone welcome a tragedy. But once it has occurred, you can know that God *will* work it together for good. He desires for you to use your tragedy as an opportunity to grow closer to Him and understand Him and His ways more. Don't push God away in bitterness. Allow yourself to draw closer to Him so He can bring you comfort and peace and walk you through the journey. It's a beautiful thing. Don't miss out on it because of bitterness and resentment.

Don't underestimate the effect you can have in people's lives by being able to identify with them in a difficult time in their life. You can be a tremendous encouragement and strength to others. In the initial weeks and months after Daniel's death, I was tremendously encouraged by talking with others who had lost a child or children. It gave me hope that I could live through it. I'm serious about that. I didn't think my heart and emotions could go on. Then I saw others who had. It gave me hope.

Who will you bring hope to? Don't let a devastating tragedy in your life be in vain. Use it to bring glory to God!

. . .

"Let your light shine before men, that they may see your good deeds and praise your Father in heaven" (Matthew 5:16).

"Rejoice in the Lord always. I will say it again: Rejoice!" (Philippians 4:4).

"Blessed are those who mourn, for they will be comforted" (Matthew 5:4).

Chapter Eleven

RODNEY'S PERSPECTIVE

(This chapter was written by Rod.)

The events surrounding the accident are moments I will never be able to forget. Even forgiveness for me seems in short supply when thinking of these moments. God is good and He has sustained us, but that day doesn't just go away. One is not whole one week, one month, or one year later. The hurt can be there ten or twenty years later. It still hurts every time I have to remember. A piece of me changed in those moments. I now believe God will fully restore me when I reach glory. It took quite some time to even believe that truth.

Things did not turn out as we had hoped. The days and weeks following the accident were very long and hard. I went through a lot of depression during the first year. A direct, divine message from God, directly to me one year after the accident, helped to change that. In spite of that, it was a very long road. There are still times when events and memories seem very difficult and troubling. It is vital for us to realize that healing really does take time. You can't expect yourself or your loved ones who have experienced tragedy or a close loss to be over it and ready to move on in life in some short amount of time. Time must be allowed for healing, without pressure to do so.

I believe true healing requires a touch from our heavenly Father. I know many individuals who have seemingly never recovered from loss. It's not easy, and it requires choices on our part to move ahead. The Bible tells us to *think about good things* (Philippians 4:8). This speaks of a choice; actually, an ongoing series of choices we must make. I know that in my own experience, I have had to choose on a daily basis what I will think or dwell on. Especially when going through a devastating loss or traumatic experience, this is sometimes a minute-by-minute series of decisions we must make. We truly must take control of our minds and choose to think on things that will assist us in overcoming tough situations. This may take a long time in some cases. We must all demonstrate love and acceptance while encouraging not only ourselves but also our family and friends in these efforts.

In the same way, we never fully understand what others are experiencing in their mind or conscience. I have wrestled with significant challenges over the decades following Daniel's passing. The Apostle Paul tells us that he too experienced troubling, long-term situations. He tells us, "To keep me from becoming conceited . . . there was given me a thorn in my flesh" (2 Corinthians 12:7). I am not going to pretend to fully understand that verse, and I certainly do not want to take it out of context. There has been great debate as to whether this was a physical "thorn," or if that was figuratively spoken. Some contend he had poor eyesight. I don't know. I do know Paul went through a lot in his life. He was persecuted, shipwrecked, injured, and ultimately martyred for his faith. (We would not have several books of the Bible had Paul not been imprisoned, which gave him the time and need to write the letters from which we now have the opportunity to learn.) Keeping all that in mind, he chose to speak of something that was an ongoing struggle for him. I relate to this on some levels. I want to share some of my thoughts and conclusions regarding a couple of the topics with which I have struggled.

. . .

Fault and Judgment

We live in a society that demands fault. It creeps into our everyday thinking and interactions. Even when we do not approach situations with that mindset, many may think we are looking for fault. It has indoctrinated our thinking. I don't believe it is consistent with the teachings of Christ, but it has certainly even become prevalent in our churches, because it is prevalent within us. The "church" is made up of individuals. When a mess is found, the first question is, "Who did that?" We want to know who is responsible. I submit for your consideration the idea that oftentimes, *it doesn't really matter.*

Here is a scenario for you to illustrate my point. Child "A" brings a glass of milk into the family room. He carefully sets the milk next to his chair and begins watching television. Child "B" comes into the room, perhaps running or jostling about. Child B is not paying attention to the fact there is a glass of milk on the floor next to a chair. Child "C" approaches the first two with his tablet to show them a funny video, and in the process, Child B or C bumps the glass, and the milk tips over. At this point, who is to blame? Child B is sure Child C knocked over the glass, and vice versa. Child A is upset his milk is spilled and feels like a bit of a victim in the whole ordeal. As Child B and C argue, they realize they can blame Child A for setting milk where it doesn't belong. As a parent hears the commotion, their first question is, "Who had milk in the family room?" Now, Child B and C are certain it isn't their fault. Child A now feels totally victimized and unjustly blamed but suddenly remembers, "Mom said not to bring drinks in the family room because we have new carpet." The entire situation turns to chaos and everyone is upset, blaming each other, and all are at odds with each other.

Meanwhile, the milk is soaking into the carpet worse and worse because . . . everyone is preoccupied with blame, and no one is dealing with the real problem: There is milk on the new carpet. All that should really matter at that moment is cleaning up the milk and mitigating the damage to the best of everyone's ability. Just imagine if all three children would jump up to grab a towel and rags as they each apologize to each other for whatever role they played in the mistake. "I'm sorry I didn't see the milk." "Oh, if I hadn't set it there, none of this would have happened." The parent could see them working together and point out that while they wish the milk hadn't spilled, the response is a good one. Does that happen? I would say it is very rare at best. We almost always seem to get caught up in blaming and justifying, don't we?

This scenario is a small word picture for you to consider. Consider how often we do that in nearly every aspect of life. When we carry these types of thoughts into already devastating and tough situations, it can be incredibly detrimental to all involved. Lifelong friendships can be ruined. A lifetime of self-loathing and self-blaming can begin. It is neither healthy nor good.

The real issue is the difference between condemnation and encouragement. Romans 8:1 tells us, "Therefore, there is now no condemnation for those who are in Christ Jesus." Luke 6:37 takes it even further in saying, "Do not judge, and you will not be judged. Do not condemn, and you will not be condemned. Forgive, and you will be forgiven." Somehow, these scriptures seem to sit in the back of our mind, brought to recall when we ourselves need forgiveness. They often seem to be related only to issues of sin and forgiveness of that sin. But honestly, are we working as agents of condemnation when the milk is spilled and all we seem to care about is who we can blame? Are we heaping coals on those we should be encouraging to clean up the mess and save the carpet? What about the "carpet" of our lives, the blame and condemnation we sometimes feel within our souls? Many times, our self-judgment is only confirmed by what we receive or perceive from others.

For me, the blame from Daniel's accident felt like it began immediately. Tammy and I stood in the emergency room and held our son after lifesaving measures were discontinued. We stood praying and begging the Lord to somehow perform a miracle. In a state of shock, pain, grief, and almost disconnected half-consciousness, we held our son who no longer had breath. Whether he entered eternity at the moment life-supportive measures were stopped or hours earlier, I cannot say. I know he was with God. *To be absent from the body is to be present with the Lord* (2 Corinthians 5:8). He was gone. We knew it, and the reality of what that meant was somewhat beginning to sink in.

More friends and family began gathering at the hospital. My grandparents, Tammy's parents, then my parents and aunt and uncle arrived. Our family gathered in a room the hospital provided for us to say our goodbyes. The nurses presented Daniel wrapped in warm blankets so we could all hold him for the last time. I tear up thinking of it now. It was so thoughtful and kind of them, and yet so hopelessly sad and pitiful to have to go through.

The phone calls began. Again, this was pre-cell phone era. The staff allowed my mother-in-law to use the landline. I will never forget overhearing a call she made to her parents' home in Ohio. I could hear her break the news. Immediately, she began explaining what had happened as best she could. (She really didn't even know.) I could tell what was being asked. "What happened?" "How did that happen?" "Who was supposed to be watching him?" "Why did he let him get near equipment?" It went on and on. Those were questions that continued for a long time. Every time confirmed a little more who was to blame for this horrible accident. Those are questions that really didn't matter and really didn't need to be asked. But that is our human nature. The reality was, the milk was spilled, and it simply needed to be cleaned up. No amount of blaming and knowing every last detail would ever put the milk back in the glass again.

If you are dealing with the loss of a loved one, people will ask questions that should not need to be asked. You have to understand that a combination of curiosity and wondering who is to blame overcomes common sense and the self-discipline to know what to ask and not ask. People have been programmed by an inquisitive and oftentimes judgmental society to ask and say things that can bring feelings of condemnation and not encouragement. If you are a family member, friend, or loved one of someone who is going through a terrible loss, guard your lips and discipline yourself in your speech. You do not have to know all the details. What your loved one needs is love, support, and encouragement.

Judgment is an interesting thing. Matthew 7:2 explains, "For in the same way you judge others, you will be judged, and with the measure you use, it will be measured to you." We do this to ourselves. I think this scripture is actually very practical in its application. As we judge and view others and their situations, we come to conclusions. We expect the exact same in return. So if I am constantly finding fault with the actions of others, I will naturally assume they in turn are finding fault with me and my actions. This is true even when they are not doing so. However, people do often tend to be less forgiving when dealing with someone who is very demanding and rarely understanding with others. This is a truth of life that we would all do well to understand. This is why I strongly want to overcome the tendency to be critical in my thinking of others. I encourage you to do the same. I need all the grace and understanding I can find. I certainly do not want judgment coming back to me from others.

The way I experienced this began when I heard the one-sided conversation in the hospital room. I assumed I knew what was being asked even though I couldn't hear both sides of the conversation. I knew what I would be thinking. Honestly, I think I would have been asking all the same questions as opposed to simply praying for and loving on the individuals experiencing the loss. Knowing that, I had to apply those same standards to myself. To not do so would make me a hypocrite. This was very difficult to overcome, but with God's and Tammy's help, I have done so, at least to some degree.

. . .

God's Will

One of the serious questions that have passed through my mind in the years since Daniel's passing involves the concept of God's will. This has been most difficult to wrap my mind around. In general, I believe God tells us His will in His Holy Scripture. That is why learning how God's Holy Word tells us to live is so important. After a basic understanding of His general will, we can then pray for what His calling is for our individual lives. But specifically, what actually was God's will in our family that seemingly awful day in September 1994? Was the Holy Spirit leading me, and did I miss His leading? With this question came guilt that can drive a person to depths of self-loathing, self-doubt, and, eventually, a true sense of self-condemnation. As with nearly any topic for which one has regrets, it is also easy to begin believing that everyone else has the same judgment for you as you have for yourself. Those are very dangerous and detrimental feelings.

In discussing these topics, I first want to cover a couple of "truths of life." The first one is that people not only have a free will, but they also make mistakes. Mistakes are certainly not always made with malice or ill intent. I have known wonderful people who have at times made seemingly minor mistakes and sometimes horrible mistakes. Occasionally, the worst consequences begin with a minor error in judgment. That does not change the long-term effects.

What does the Bible actually say about God's will? How do we reconcile scripture with what we like to believe; namely, the idea that once we put our faith in the saving grace of Christ, all will be good, and we should have no real problems anymore? If we do still have problems, we assume we have somehow messed up, because a loving Father would never allow his children to suffer. Therefore, ultimately . . . all of our problems are our fault. There's that word again, "fault." We're still looking for a place to lay blame, and ultimately it's up to us and our faith or lack of faith to make our own life great! To that, I say, "Bologna!"

First of all, I do not presume to always know the will of God for each specific situation. While we are told in 1 Corinthians 2:16 that if we are believers in the Lord Jesus, we have the mind of Christ, this is not the equivalent of always knowing the perfect will of a sovereign God. In regards to when the second coming of the Messiah will take place, Mark 13:32 tells us, "No one knows about that day or hour, not even the angels in heaven, nor the Son, but only the Father.'" In this passage, scripture clearly tells us that this detail is even hidden from Christ Himself. No one, including the Son (Jesus Christ), knows the hour or the day of the Lord's return. We are told that He is ready to return, but He is waiting on the Father's command. Scripture does not say this is the only thing hidden from Christ. I don't know if there are other things, but if the Father has not revealed this one, it seems reasonable He has perhaps hidden other mysteries. How, then, we could think we would always know God's will for every circumstance when Christ Himself doesn't know every last detail is beyond me. I think that is presumptuous and void of a basic understanding of who we are and who God is. I do believe we are able to have a sense of the Father's nature. But anything we do, say, and believe is supposed to be wholly based on the Father and His plan. Jesus Himself told His followers, "'The Son can do . . . only what he sees his Father doing'" (John 5:19).

I want to reference three aspects of God's will.

First is God's general will: God has a general will that He would like for us. This is explained and taught through studying His Holy Scriptures. Yet, He designed us with a free will which He allows us to exercise. Among many choices we have with our free will, we have a choice to trust Him or blame Him. To better understand His will for us, we can refer to many scriptures that portray His plans for how we should live life.

Second, God's sovereign will: We can see in scripture many times where He has spoken and what He has spoken simply happens because He has spoken it. Consider creation. Look, too, at Christ dying for the sins of all mankind.

That was the avenue with which God designed our freedom from sin and death. Our freedom comes no other way.

Third, God's apparent willingness to change His mind at our request: There are times where God has demonstrated a willingness to change how something will happen, seemingly changing the outcome of the future. A key point to understand is that our request to the Lord must still line up with the overall will of the Father as demonstrated in scripture. You will find examples in Genesis 19 concerning Abraham and Lot, and in John 2 when Jesus turned water to wine.

I wish I always knew the will of the Father, yet I don't. I see things through my own eyes and through my earthly understanding and desires. The Lord tells us, "'My ways (are) higher than your ways and my thoughts than your thoughts'" (Isaiah 55:9). I truly want to have the understanding of the Lord, and I do ask for that understanding, but I must have more confidence in His plan and His blessing for eternity than my own. Why is it that I can trust Him with eternity, but have such a lack of faith for the details of today?

. . .

Not Intended to Deal with Loss/Death

Another truth of life I believe God has revealed addresses why we deal so poorly with death in the first place. I remember the day I received this understanding. It was life-changing, if for no other reason than simply for the sake of understanding how we are lovingly made. I do not like death, and I never will like something so seemingly final and destructive. I believe the Lord showed me it's more than all right that I don't like death. In fact, it is appropriate that I hate death. God never made us to understand or to feel accepting and fine with the concept of death!

Man was created to be eternal. It was not until sin came through Adam and Eve and they were exiled from the Garden of Eden that death even came into the picture. Mankind was created to live forever in fellowship with God. While our bodies are now temporary fixtures of this fallen world, our soul and spirit are eternal. The real essence of who we are never passes away. Although the body dies, the real us lives on through our soul and spirit. This is one of the reasons we find ourselves groping around, searching for some explanation to make loss seem all right and even good. We look for explanations that allow us to reason out in our own minds why it is all right for our elderly grandparent to become ill and pass, but it is tragic if this happens to a youth or middle-aged person. We may even go so far as to twist scripture into something that helps us explain away, in our own minds and to others, losses that are so impactful to our lives.

Think of the implications of this fact: the real us was never intended to experience death, neither that of others or our own. Therefore, the real us, our soul and spirit, doesn't even begin to understand this separation we all experience through the death of a loved one. We were NEVER intended to experience or understand this thing we call death, and therefore we do not deal well with death. *It simply wasn't part of the original plan.*

Fortunately, we have a loving Creator who redeemed even death and turned it into the doorway to an eternity with Him. What a wonderful gift—one that helps us cope with our feelings of sorrow and separation. But make no mistake about it; it was not the plan. It is wonderful that we can combat these feelings by thinking on what is right, pure, and just (Philippians 4:8) and choosing to focus on the great hope (Titus 1:2) we have in our Lord God through Christ our Savior. In spite of all this, our soul and spirit were never intended to deal with such great loss.

. . .

Comfort, Challenge, and Healing

My healing took a great amount of time. It was encouraged and supported in a number of ways through many individuals. The Holy Spirit is there to lead us and to guide us in our daily walk. That includes our interactions with others, through good times and difficult times. God's Spirit may lead you in a particular interaction you should have with someone who has experienced a great loss. We must keep in mind that when we are truly led by the Spirit of God, we can participate in the healing process God wants to accomplish in the life of another. When we do these things on our own, without God, it may not be part of His plan and may not prove to be healing. Timing is so very important in all we do in, through, and for the Lord.

On the long drive home from the hospital in Kalamazoo that September evening, I had already begun questioning everything about life. I was replaying not only the decisions of that day, but also many decisions that led up to that day and its events. Tom Tison, a good friend, was chauffeuring me in our car as we headed south. I can only imagine the sound of the babble coming from my mouth . . . really coming from my soul. Tom was gracious and allowed me to ramble. At one point, I began questioning the entire process of securing land, building our own home, and all the decisions that went into the process. Tom very gently encouraged me with the challenge that I should not question everything I had done in life that led up to the moments of the accident. That challenge has stuck with me in life and has encouraged me in many other situations since. It was an appropriate, caring challenge from a good friend. His timing was perfect, and his wisdom was invaluable.

Uncle Paul Chupp and his son Ruben called each Sunday morning for many months to ask how they could pray for us that day with their church congregations. Both were pastors of congregations we were not part of. Yet we were a part of them through the body of Christ, and they understood Romans 12:15 that instructs us to "rejoice with those who rejoice; mourn with those who mourn." There was a special comfort each time one of them would call. First of all, we knew they really cared as they took the time to stay in contact with us. Secondly, we knew their church congregations were in prayer over our family. God's people were standing with us and praying for us regularly. What a comfort to consider! Those calls went on for quite some time, perhaps a year or longer.

We have good friends named Jim and Julie Taylor who ministered to us in several ways. We were co-leaders of a junior high youth group in our congregation when the accident occurred. Naturally, the youth had spent a great deal of time with Daniel because he usually went to the meetings with us. They loved him very much. One evening we arrived home to find a paper bag hanging near the entrance of our home. In it were homemade notes, cards, and letters from the members of our youth group. Julie, an incredible artist, had taken the time to collect supplies, allowing the children to bless us with the special handmade cards, as well as taking a step in their own healing. We sat and cried as we read the comments of love and concern from those young people. What a blessing it was.

On Sunday mornings, holding Daniel while singing songs during our worship service had been such a special time. It was another thing that was very difficult after his passing. On several occasions, I would exit the rear of the sanctuary when overcome by grief. One week, shortly after making my exit, Jim came out the back door behind me. He had care and concern in his eyes. He inquired if I was all right and asked if he could do anything to help. This seemingly simple act from a friend was incredibly helpful, and I appreciate it to this day. Again, knowing the care and concern Jim had for me was healing in and of itself.

Sometime later, as I continued to struggle during times of worship, I went out back and down the hallway. I was near the front entrance when my uncle Floyd Miller approached me from behind. As I turned around, he spoke to me with a stern sound. He had a bit of a quiver in his voice and almost a tremble to his body. He got very close and looked me right in the eyes.

You have to understand this was very out of character for my uncle. He is very wise, but is also very meek and quiet. He doesn't often offer advice unless it is first sought out. Therefore, he would have been one of the last people I would have expected to meet me in the hall for a confrontation. I spent a lot of time at my uncle's house while growing up. My cousins were like brothers to me, and my uncle and aunt were like second parents. We had a good relationship. I trusted him. I knew that he would genuinely have my best interest in mind.

There we were in the hallway. My uncle was kind of in my face, and both of us were uptight. I was crying and feeling so bad about what had happened with Daniel. Uncle Floyd was shook up because of what he was about to do.

"Stop it!" he said.

I stared at him and he again said, "Stop it!" I told him I was sorry, so sorry.

He told me, "You have nothing to be sorry about." Then, he uttered life-changing words. He said, "Right now, you're no good to anyone. You're no good to your wife. You're no good to your new baby. You're no good to anyone. Stop it!"

Needless to say, this took me aback. I had not experienced a rebuke in my situation. Until that point, I had received love and care in the form of comforting words from family and friends. This was different. It called me to take responsibility, to move on, and to make a decision to change my behavior, outlook, and way of responding to the most life-shaking event I had ever experienced at that point in my life. My humble uncle was *calling me out*, so to speak. Those comments were made in love and care in the form of a great challenge. *"As iron sharpens iron, so one person sharpens another"* (Proverbs 27:17).

Interestingly, both gentlemen I mentioned above had *a word from the Lord* for me. Both had timely comments that ministered love and care at very important times in my life. Had Jim confronted me with a somewhat harsh challenge, I wouldn't have been ready to receive such a rebuke at that time. On the other hand, if Uncle Floyd had simply offered me sympathy, I may not have chosen to move on through the process of once again becoming a healthy, whole person. All four of the examples I shared display how we all must be led by the Spirit of God. There are times when we feel we can clearly see what someone else needs to know. We need to ask ourselves if it is our place and if it's the right time for us to share our thoughts. Having a relationship that allowed me to appreciate the wisdom from my uncle was also very key. Again, I knew he had nothing but my best in mind. I fully appreciate each gesture related in these four stories. I believe they all stemmed from a leading from the Lord.

A clear sense of how God would have us to love others is so very important.

The Red Ball

The struggle to deal with great loss can seem like a continual thorn with which we battle. Sometimes it is a date, a particular time of day, or a unique situation that presents itself. I had many of these situations following Daniel's passing. I still do from time to time. For the longest time, I couldn't watch and enjoy college football. The day Daniel passed was the start of the college football season, and even though he was very young, I fully intended on sharing "opening day" with my son. Labor Day weekend is still bittersweet and probably always will be. These are real issues with which we are challenged.

One such experience that brought back an unexpected rush of emotions was what I'll call the "Red Ball Experience." If you recall, the day of the accident included Daniel playing with our fun-loving dog, Auggie. While Daniel was playing with Auggie, he was also playing with a mid-sized red ball. Daniel would throw the ball, and Auggie would run after it. This was an activity that seemed to keep them both occupied and happy. I looked over several times toward Daniel and enjoyed seeing this playful activity. Life was good, all the way around.

Fast forward to a cool fall Friday evening. My Uncle Merlin and his children had asked if they could come over to the house to help us plant our lawn the next day. It had been some time and I had not tackled this challenge; partly because I didn't want to do much, and partly because I honestly was not excited about going out to *that lawn* and working where my son was injured. The second was more significant than I realized at the time. We set a time for Saturday morning. While I was very happy for the help, I was not looking forward to the tasks we would be tackling.

I had several things I needed to accomplish before we were ready to pull the drag, level the soil, collect the rocks we turned up, sow the grass seed, and spread the straw. There were some things in the yard area that needed to be moved. One such item was our dog house. Having the dog house seemed a bit unnecessary since we had the barn. Auggie would lie in the barn when outdoors for the night or at the foot of the basement steps when inside the house. However, we kept it around partially out of sentiment. I had built it while still in high school. We also thought we may need it again one day.

I decided to move the dog house, which weighed about 250 pounds. As I tried to wrestle it, one end at a time, something quite unexpected happened. I lifted on the rear end, leaving the front end on the ground. To my surprise, out rolled the red ball. *The* red ball. *Daniel's* red ball! I released the weight of the heavy structure from my hands and stared at the ball. I walked over and picked it up. As I stood there holding his beloved toy, I began to weep uncontrollably. A flood of emotions came rushing in for which I felt completely unprepared. It caught me off guard, as I was certainly not expecting to see that memorable ball.

Earlier in our effort to "get on with life," Tammy had cleaned things that Daniel left dirty. We had put his toys away and washed the last of his soiled clothes. A few times, I had actually wondered where his red ball with the faded smiley face on it had disappeared to. Time passed. When I least expected it, this happened. I stood and cried as I thought of the last time he played with the ball. I thought about the fact he would never do that again. I so wished I could witness his innocent play once more. I contemplated, was he on his way to get my attention because he couldn't get the ball out from within the dog house? No, surely not. He had climbed in and out of the dog house in his play many times that day. All of these thoughts barraged my mind. I had no answers. At that point, everything was very fresh again.

I wasn't choosing to wallow in self-pity or distrust of God. It did cause me to again feel much of the pain I had previously felt. Several questions came to mind. *How could this have happened? God, where were You . . . where are You?* God was gracious. He was up for the questions and the emotional reaction. Tammy, of course, didn't know what was going on when I returned to the house depressed and without any desire to communicate, but she too was gracious when I finally spit out what had happened. With prayer and the faith we had deep inside, we pressed on.

Those types of things happen. Those times come. I assure you, God is a big, strong, loving God who can handle those situations. While at that moment I felt as though I had not progressed in my healing, the reality was that I had. That experience brought a little more healing—over time. I suspect the Lord allowed me the red ball experience when He knew I could handle it. It was tough, but I sure treasured finding that ball. I took it inside and saved it as it took on a new special meaning to me.

Whether it is you who have suffered a loss or someone you know, it is all right to have those moments. Those moments enable the grieving process to move along and assist us in not repressing feelings and questions. These times are normal and all right. Remember to go to God in these times. He is more than capable of holding, loving, and sustaining you.

. . .

"Be strong and courageous. Do not be afraid or terrified because of them, for the Lord your God goes with you; he will never leave you nor forsake you" (Deuteronomy 31:6).

"'As the heavens are higher than the earth, so are my ways higher than your ways and my thoughts than your thoughts'" (Isaiah 55:9).

"And my God will meet all your needs according to the riches of his glory in Christ Jesus" (Philippians 4:19).

Chapter Twelve

LIFE'S UPS AND DOWNS

(The remainder of this book is written by Tammy.)

When Chris was in kindergarten, I began volunteering at our local public elementary school, one day each week. My dad, who still worked second shift, was available during the early part of the day and would watch Becca and Justus for me while I was at the school. I loved those days. I was able to be busy with tasks, which I loved. But more importantly, I had many opportunities to tell the students the positive things I saw in them, encourage them and the teachers in various ways, and sometimes share my story. Yes, there were times when one of the teachers and I would both be in tears. In the end, I could bring it back around to God's faithfulness in my life. I had that wonderful blessing and opportunity for twelve years. I cherish those days at Centreville Elementary.

Though God had done a wonderful healing in my life, I still had seasons of sadness and difficulty. The summer Daniel would have turned thirteen, I struggled a great deal. Our son Chris was on a baseball team with his three cousins Josh, Jonathan, and Drew. All summer, I mourned for what should have been. Daniel *should have been* on that team. It was a difficult year for me. I *should have been* celebrating being the mom of a teenager. I *should have had* a junior high student. I *should have had* four school-aged children . . . I got ripped off!

That's what I dealt with all summer long as I mourned for what *should have been*. I'm not sure if there was a connection, but the following winter I was unexpectedly diagnosed with depression. How unpredictable that I went more than twelve years without struggling with clinical depression, and it was moving in on me now. This time, medication was recommended to me. I resisted that even though I knew I was in bad shape. I was anxious, overwhelmed, discouraged, had a negative attitude, and I wasn't sleeping well. I thought I was just stressed out. My doctor talked me into trying antidepressants for si weeks. She said I could stop taking them if I didn't feel they were helping. At last I decided to take them so I could prove her wrong.

She was right. Three weeks into taking the antidepressants, I had a good day. It felt strange to me. A few days later, I had another good day, and that became the norm. At that point, I realized how long it had been since I had had a "good day." I likely had been mildly depressed for years and didn't realize it. It was so nice to feel good again.

I share that part of my story because I want people to understand that sometimes antidepressants are necessary. One should never feel weak or guilty for needing them. They were a lifesaver for me. They truly helped me make it through another difficult season in my life. I am no longer on antidepressants. Some people need them long-term. Never judge anyone who struggles with clinical depression. It is a very dark, lonely, and overwhelming place to be. Rejoice if you have never had to deal with it. You are truly blessed.

I struggle with Seasonal Affective Disorder (SAD). It usually hits me in the late winter months. Sometimes I can get through a whole winter without it being much of a problem. Other times, it hits me in the fall and I deal with it all winter long. When I begin to feel the symptoms, I know I need to focus more on eating healthy whole foods, getting plenty of rest, getting out in the sunlight if possible, drinking plenty of water, continuing to get regular exercise and activity, and taking specific nutritional supplements. Some people go to tanning beds to help with SAD. I have done that when it has seemed really bad, and it does help. I take supplements such as red clover, black cohash, and ginseng that are mood elevating, help fight off stress, and positively affect hormone levels. Vitamin D is really important too. As always, God is faithful to direct me through those times and give me wisdom as to which measures to take.

. . .

Two thousand ten to eleven would have been Daniel's senior year in high school. We should have been planning a graduation party as we looked through all of his school memories. But there was nothing to sort through. It wasn't to be. Instead, we watched our friends and other proud parents prepare their eighteen-year-olds for the next phase of their life. Did they have any idea how fortunate they were? Again, it was a very difficult year, but the fact remained that I knew God had brought an amazing level of healing to my heart and mind. At least these episodes of sadness were just seasons, not a constant for me anymore. It had been five years since I had really struggled with the feelings of mourning what should have been. Thank God for that.

2011

• • •

As I write this, it has been five years since my last significant mourning episode. I do have moments of sadness from time to time, but thank God, they are fleeting. Rod and I continue to move forward with life as God brings it. We can't focus on what should have been, so we focus on what we have. In many ways, life is better than we expected it to be. We have three delightful teen-to-young adult children, who are a wonderful blessing. I can honestly say, "Life is good!" I have loved having teenagers.

Currently (spring of 2016), at age twenty-one, Chris is a very responsible college senior. He is enjoying an internship and working toward a Master of Science degree in Accountancy, ultimately planning to have a career as a CPA. He is very focused and driven. Eighteen-year-old Becca graduated from high school and junior college in spring of 2015 and is finishing her junior year in college to obtain a business degree. She loves anything related to math and hopes to work with a non-profit organization so she can mentor youth. Justus, at age sixteen, is a carefree, yet very busy, high school sophomore enjoying life. He has begun taking a few college credits and is on track to have an associate degree one year after high school graduation. He has a love for basketball, running, and doing anything creative. It pleases me most that our children have all made a decision to serve God and follow His lead in their life. Rod and I are very proud of them and feel so incredibly blessed.

God has redeemed our pain. We walk with Him daily and trust Him to guide us. He always does. I believe He always will.

February 2016

• • •

As I reflect on life's ups and downs, a real-life analogy comes to mind. My aunt Melva beautifully decorated her Christmas tree. One morning she found her tree lying on the living room floor in disarray, with broken ornaments. It was quite a mess. Naturally, she was discouraged and, frankly, overwhelmed. She had to temporarily walk away from the debris. Later that day, she and her husband were able to carefully take hold of the tree, and together they stood it up. They cleaned up the broken pieces, swept up the pine needles, and tediously rearranged the decorations on the tree. Once again, after much ado, the tree was restored to its original beauty. It wasn't the same as before, yet it was just as lovely.

The image this story brings to mind is that sometimes life gets messy in unexpected ways. When things come crashing down, we have some choices. Will we look at the mess and decide it's not worth trying to fix? I hope not. It may seem overwhelming at first, but working toward making something right or improved is certainly better than just letting it go. Who wants to look at a fallen down, non-lit Christmas tree, right? If we become so disappointed and upset that we think, "Forget it! I can't handle this!"—well, the mess and broken pieces won't go away. They either have to be put back into place, or they eventually have to be picked up and thrown away. Leaving the mess in a heap would be even more discouraging and depressing.

Another thing we may have to ask ourselves is, "Am I going to take care of it right away or later?" Well, sometimes we don't have time to deal with things right away. In that case, it's okay to postpone it for a short time. A healthy decision is to take care of it—the sooner the better.

When we choose to finally get started and put the pieces back together, we have to realize that it takes time, patience, and effort. It took a lot more time to put that tree back together than it took for it to fall over. Oftentimes our messes, heartaches, and devastating circumstances can happen in an instant. It may take months or years to pick ourselves up and put the pieces back together. Often, it requires assistance from others to aid us, bring encouragement, and help us to hope for restoration once again.

Don't look at a mess and wonder, "How am I possibly going to take care of this?" Instead, go to your closest loved ones and ask for help or perspective. When others help us, it not only feels less overwhelming, but it goes more quickly, and their perspective can be invaluable.

Have you ever looked all over for a hat or pair of glasses only to have someone inform you that your lost item is on your head? Sometimes, other people can see things in a different way than we can. What seems impossible to us may seem obvious and simple to someone else. That is why it is imperative to depend on others to help us walk through our toughest times.

We have a large, supportive family, and we have also been connected to many wonderful believers through our church relationships. They prayed for us, brought us meals, sent encouraging notes, or called us to speak life and hope into us. I know many times it was by the prompting of the Holy Spirit. We felt loved and cared for. Nanci Schwartz did that beautifully for us. For years we would get a card or a plate of cookies on Daniel's birthday and the day he died. She would often write a meaningful note to let us know she was thinking of us. I think that ministry is invaluable. It meant the world to us. To know someone remembered was priceless. It inspired me to do that for others. I make note of special days. I put them in my calendar so I remember from year to year. If nothing else, I pray for those who lost a loved one.

We experienced something else that was a new feeling to us. We felt prayed for. It's true. We could feel ourselves being lifted by the prayers of those who circled around us in support. What an awesome feeling.

Sometimes in these situations, the crushing circumstances also distress our closest circles of support. In our case, both Rod's and my parents lost their only grandchild. Our siblings lost their only nephew. Two sets of our grandparents lost their only great-grandchild. They were also deeply hurting. They had their own pain to deal with, but they also felt a great deal of pain on our behalf. We were all struggling in different ways. Because of that, we needed to broaden our circle of support. We needed to draw from outside resources and widen our base of strength.

We, along with our church friends, firmly believed God answers prayer and miracles can happen. We still believe that. When Daniel died after much prayer in faith, many of our church friends were also traumatized, especially the junior high youth group we led. The grief was widespread. It affected every circle we were a part of in one way or another.

. . .

I sensed a certain level of grace to walk through what we were going through. I think God gives us grace to endure the hardships He allows in our lives. Many people have asked how we could endure such pain and tragedy. They have even expressed that they themselves would not have been able to cope with it. That's what I thought before it happened. I soon knew what grace felt like. It was God that helped us walk through our tragedy, and His grace that carried us.

Receiving grace for a difficult situation is an interesting thing. Let me demonstrate it with a word picture. You only need a life preserver when you are struggling to stay afloat. People on the shore who may be seeing you struggle might feel anxiety, stress, or even pain as they see you struggle, but they are not the ones who need the life preserver. They might imagine how awful it is for you to be struggling to breathe, but they don't need the life preserver. I think God's grace works in a similar way. When you go through a tragedy, you really need the grace of God to carry you through it. He gives us that grace when we need it. The people who are watching the struggle don't need that same grace, and they don't receive that same measure of grace. Therefore, it's difficult for them to imagine how one can bear that pain. Thank God for His grace when we need it.

Life has its ups and downs, its hills and valleys. When you are in a valley, know that if you keep walking, you will eventually get to a hill. Hang in there and make healthy emotional choices. Things will eventually get better.

. . .

"I waited patiently for the Lord; he turned to me and heard my cry. He lifted me out of the slimy pit, out of the mud and mire; he set my feet on a rock and gave me a firm place to stand. He put a new song in my mouth, a hymn of praise to our God. Many will see and fear the Lord and put their trust in him" (Psalm 40:1-2).

"The Sovereign Lord is my strength; he makes my feet like the feet of a deer, he enables me to tread on the heights" (Habakkuk 3:19).

"For who is God besides the Lord? And who is the Rock except our God? It is God who arms me with strength and keeps my way secure. He makes my feet like the feet of a deer; he causes me to stand on the heights" (Psalm 18:31-33).

Chapter Thirteen

LIFE LESSONS

I have learned a lot about pain, grief, and loss over the past few decades. I have grown tremendously in my understanding of God. I hope I have adequately shared with you the hope of renewed life and joy after hardship, tragedy, trials, or loss. I purposed to be very candid about the difficulty of loss, but I especially want to bring you back around to hope and redemption.

Shortly after Daniel died, a neighbor gave me the book When Life is Changed Forever by Rick Taylor. It was revolutionary to jump-start my healing process. I needed desperately to identify with someone. Rick and Judy's story helped me tremendously to relate to them. It helped answer several questions, and helped me make sense out of some things. It brought hope to me while my life seemed upside down.

Everyone has disappointments, tragedies, hurts, failures, and trials at some point in their life. The Bible tells us that we have an enemy called the devil. He wants to hurt us, throw us off track, get us to blame God for things that He didn't do and cause discouragement in our lives. In fact, 1 Peter 5:8 says, "Be alert and of sober mind. Your enemy the devil prowls around like a roaring lion looking for someone to devour." John 10:10 reminds us, "'The thief comes only to steal and kill and destroy; I have come that they may have life, and have it to the full.'" Another favorite scripture of mine is Genesis 50:20: "You (the devil) intended to harm me, but God intended it for good to accomplish what is now being done, the saving of many lives.'" One more from Romans 8:28 says, "And we know that in all things God works for the good of those who love him, who have been called according to his purpose."

The devil likes to trip us up. God turns things around for our good. Chapter 34 of Job tells us that it is impossible for God to do anything evil or wicked. Yet He does allow things to happen that we don't like. Sometimes those very things are results of choices we have made.

If you are trying to make sense of a tragedy or trial, don't. It is usually pretty impossible to make good sense out of something terrible that happens to us. How could anything good possibly come from the death of a loved one? That is a very difficult thing to process, and it most often will never make sense to us.

When Daniel died, we didn't look at the situation and think, "Oh yes, God has allowed this to happen because He will use us down the road to bring hope and comfort to others." No, we didn't even to begin to think such a thing. Yet that is exactly what God has done. Had we never experienced the death of a close loved one, we still would not be able to truly relate to those who have.

God has opened many doors over the years for us to share with families who have lost a child. For some, it was simply interceding for them in prayer. For others it was talking with them, bringing comfort and a message of hope by demonstrating how we were making it though it was a very difficult journey. There have been some that we have spent hours with whose struggle was deeper or difficult to pull through. I love being only a phone call or a text away from encouraging someone through the truth of God's Word, or praying for them. At times, I have dropped everything to go be with someone who is going through an intense struggle. I know that consuming feeling. It can feel dark and hopeless. But it doesn't have to. There really is life and hope on the other side of devastating loss. Aah, yes. Hope and life!

I have shared our testimony through various venues. When God opens a door, I am more than happy to walk through it if it brings blessing and hope to someone.

If you have endured a devastating season or event in your life, be assured of one thing. If you love God and turn to Him, He will heal you, in time, and He will turn your situation around to be used for good. Isn't that wonderful news? Rest in the Lord, allow yourself to heal, and give it some time. At some point, you want to be ready and able to be a blessing to others. It is really difficult to do that when you are still deeply wounded. Don't put pressure on yourself to encourage someone when you yourself need to be encouraged.

When you do feel as though God has brought a significant amount of healing to your hurting heart, be aware of doors that He may be opening for you. He will lead you.

. . .

Early in 2014, God put it on my heart to write my story in the form of a book, to share it with many more people. Initially, I waited for confirmation. I have never considered myself a writer, especially a book writer. I struggled to keep mediocre grades in my English, reading, and literature classes in high school. I never imagined myself writing a book, nor has it ever been even a faint dream. I have walked through this process only through obedience to God and to bring glory to Him. I pray God can use this book and our story to minister to someone's heart.

. . .

My prayer for those of you who have experienced a loss is to accomplish what Dr. Taylor did for me. I want you to have someone to relate to so you know your feelings and thoughts are normal. I hope to have settled some questions in your mind. And most of all, I pray I brought you hope!

For those of you who have not experienced the death of someone close, my prayer is this book helped to shed light on how to relate to those who have. I hope that you have a deeper understanding of how to reach out to them, how to pray for them, what to say to them, and how to encourage them in their healing.

Healing is a process. Sometimes it's a long process. Perhaps that's why it took twenty years for God to prompt me to pen my story. Speaking of twenty years—to this day, God continues to fulfill the word He spoke over Daniel at his baby dedication. His life (and death) has impacted many people for the kingdom of God. Because of his death, our testimony has impacted and influenced the hearts of people, and many people have come to know the goodness and grace of God. ***Praise be to God! He is faithful and sovereign!***

What is it that you are struggling with the most? Take it to God. Go to the scriptures. Don't just take someone's word for it. God wants to minister to your heart, answer your questions, and revolutionize how you see and understand Him. He is faithful and sovereign. I promise you that! But don't just take my word for it. Seek Him for yourself.

. . .

"May the God of hope fill you with all joy and peace as you trust in him, so that you may overflow with hope by the power of the Holy Spirit" (Romans 15:13).

"I can do all this through him who gives me strength" (Philippians 4:13).

"Do not fear, for I have redeemed you; I have summoned you by name; you are mine. When you pass through the waters, I will be with you; and when you pass through the rivers, they will not sweep over you. When you walk through the fire, you will not be burned; the flames will not set you ablaze. For I am the Lord *your God, the Holy One of Israel, your Savior"* (Isaiah 43:1b-3a).

Many blessings to you!

APPENDIX A

My written words that were read at Daniel's funeral.

Daniel was my baby. He was Rod's dream of a perfect son. He meant everything to us. We learned so much from him, not only in parenting but in teaching us how to have fun in life and that every minute counts.

I'll never forget all the little things he did. He would hide behind chairs and peek his head out to see if anyone was looking. He would scoot back on his little rocking chair with such a big smile. He wanted everyone to know what he was doing because he knew he was special. He would rock himself, then get down and come give me a kiss and hug. He would dance around the room, turning in circles. He would push his little finger in his mouth to push in food or even juice when he was eating. He would hang on tight to the sides of the wagon when I gave him rides, as he watched and laughed at Auggie following behind. And, of course, we can't forget him holding his own hair to comfort himself when he was tired or sad.

Whatever Daniel did, he made up his mind he was going to have fun, and he did. He brought joy to everyone he met, and touched their lives. He certainly touched my life.

There are so many questions we can ask, but it is not for us to question God, just try to accept what He has allowed. Don't question why or how. Don't blame anyone. We don't . . . and we can't. We can't change what happened. The only thing we can change is our future, and how precious we hold and cherish the loved ones we have now. Parents, cherish every minute you get to spend with your kids.

I always thought I loved Daniel more than anything, and I could never handle losing him. God has shown me we can live even without our most prized earthly possessions. God has been faithful. He is my strength and my rock. He is my fortress and deliverer. In Him I will always trust.

I love our God. I love Him more than anything. He will bring us through this.

God didn't take Daniel from us. I choose to believe He gave him to us for 13½ of the best months of my life. Thank You, God. Thank You for such a precious, irreplaceable gift that You trusted us with for a whole year.

We *will* go on because God will help us through this. Only through God do we have the strength. God's grace is sufficient.

Remember Daniel . . . hugging Jesus, patting Him on the back, then giving Him a kiss. Jesus must be so happy.

—Written September 4, 1994

APPENDIX B

The symptoms of PTSD may include flashbacks, bad dreams or thoughts, feeling numb, avoiding places or things that trigger memories, guilt, depression, worry, losing interest in activities, and other symptoms. If you are dealing with symptoms like these, it would be a wise to see a doctor to discuss treatment options. Medication, "talk" therapy, or both may help. For more information on PTSD or depression, go to the website for the National Institute of Mental Health.

ABOUT THE AUTHOR

Tammy has been married to Rodney Chupp since 1991. They have four children. She works part time for a home health care agency and is on staff at Riverside Church, where her family attends. She has a passion for seeing people grow in their knowledge of God, understand His will for their life, and understand how to recognize His voice. She speaks, teaches, and shares God's heart at women's events and daily in the divine appointments God brings her way.

She loves to encourage people through her Facebook page "Threads of Faith," where she shares scripturally based thoughts and stories to encourage others.

She is part of a weekly Celebrate Recovery ministry that takes a Christ-centered recovery program to the St. Joseph County Jail.

She walks in her purpose and calling.

If you would like to contact me, leave a message on my "Threads of Faith" Facebook page.

CPSIA information can be obtained
at www.ICGtesting.com
Printed in the USA
FFOW05n2042290816